Kirstie Sneyd
Returning well

Kirstie Sneyd

Returning well

———

A guide for working parents and their managers

DE GRUYTER

ISBN 978-3-11-161827-2
e-ISBN (PDF) 978-3-11-161845-6
e-ISBN (EPUB) 978-3-11-161866-1

Library of Congress Control Number: 2024950697

Bibliographic information published by the Deutsche Nationalbibliothek
The Deutsche Nationalbibliothek lists this publication in the Deutsche Nationalbibliografie;
detailed bibliographic data are available on the internet at http://dnb.dnb.de.

www.degruyter.com
Questions about General Product Safety Regulation:
productsafety@degruyterbrill.com

Praise for *Returning well*

We wouldn't have expected anything less than this book from Kirstie. She is a fabulous coach, and this book generously shares her huge experience in supporting working parents to return well. At last Kirstie brings a book on this subject that looks at the process of parental leave through a truly systemic lens, the parents, the managers, the organisation and social narratives and expectations are all included. It does all this whilst remaining incredibly rich in human story and experience and brilliantly practical with helpful checklists and accessible theory. Get it for any working parent you know, their managers and their HR departments.

Sharon Charlton-Thomson, Co-founder & Head of Coaching, The working parent company

Practical – a must have guide for the shelf of every HR professional, manager, leaver and returner. Checklists are a game-changer.

Michael Knott, Senior Practice Director, Slater & Gordon Lawyers

Returning well is a well-researched and thoughtfully written guide that offers practical advice and support for working parents and their managers. Personally, I wish I'd read it when I left to have my first baby as the resources and checklists are very useful. Having returned to work 10 months ago, I still found it valuable and will be using it as a manager of people going forwards. For anyone looking to navigate the complexities of returning to work after parental leave, I highly recommend.

Laura Magee, Associate Partner, Argon & Co

For Professionals, if you care deeply about both your family and your career and seek long-term happiness through work, then put this book on your required reading list. For Employers, you will learn to empower your team with the necessary tools to have them return to work and be happy and productive. I wish I had this book 20 years ago when I returned to work after the birth of my eldest son. Kirstie Sneyd uses knowledge, research and her own personal experience to guide employees and employers through the emotionally difficult task of returning to work after the birth of a child and an extended period off. The book is very well organized, easy to read and set up to "skip" to the areas one is most interested in.

Rosemarie Iorio, Director, Payor Solutions at Labcorp

https://doi.org/10.1515/9783111618456-202

This is the book I wished I had by my side when I returned to work after having my children. A helpful mix of practical advice and science-based evidence with a bit of positive cheerleading thrown in, all designed to help parents 'return well'.

Rebecca Birkbeck, Director Community & Membership Participation, Co-op

This book should be everybody's Bible of how to do things right. Kirstie leaves no stone unturned on what to consider for a new parent departing and returning to the workplace. It's so important to get it right for everyone involved. Brilliant work!

Liza Rabaiotti, People support lead, Stantec

The topic of leaves (and returns) has become a critical component of the broader employee experience. This is a timely book on this important topic. Providing information for different stakeholders – leavers, managers, HR and the broader organization – is particularly valuable.

Bernard Tubiana, Principal, Deloitte Consulting

Kirstie has provided exceptional support in her work with our business. She is a first-class communicator, able to build trust in challenging circumstances and get to the heart of issues with a rare sensitivity. She has a fantastic insight into the complex interpersonal dynamics of the workplace and can provide practical guidance for leadership and team members alike. This book is a great example of Kirstie's insight, providing an invaluable guide to those returning to the workplace whether that's as a parent, a manager or within the People team.

Tom Weston, Chief People Officer, Inside Travel Group

As many parents struggle between fulfilling their intellectual potential and following their parenting instincts, *Returning well* combines pragmatic suggestions with well-rounded research to offer valuable guidance to every parent looking to achieve the right work-life balance.

Clare Marchant, DBE, Vice Chancellor, University of Gloucestershire

An extremely valuable book helping parents and managers to navigate the emotionally and practically challenging issue of returning to work after having a child. Incredibly accessible and practical, balancing useful checklists and simple to understand models with an empathetic and empowering approach. A must read for any parent returning to work after parental leave.

Bethan Brookes, Coach support & development manager, Parent Gym

This is an immensely helpful guide. I thoroughly recommend it to anyone embarking on parental leave – and their managers. Kirstie skilfully condenses 25 years' coaching experience and solid research into a hugely readable, down-to-earth guide.

Harriet Beveridge, Co-author of "Will it make the boat go faster"

Wall Street employers and employees have never been great at managing leave. This book should be mandatory reading. *Returning well* provides a road map and planning tools that can be applied to maternity or any leave (planned or unplanned). Kirstie Sneyd steers clear of consulting hype terms and focusses on fact-based examples. I am putting some of these tools to work immediately!

Chris Thorpe, Chartered Financial Analyst

Kirstie is an absolute authority on this subject. Her advice reassures and empowers parents, who often experience a range of emotions about their leave and return. The book acknowledges these emotions throughout, normalising them and providing support and advice on how to manage or reframe them. Many of my clients, who are academics and research leaders, have had coaching sessions with her to help them effectively and confidently plan their parental leave and return. I'm so pleased that Kirstie's support and advice are now accessible and captured in this excellent book. *Returning well* is engaging and easy to read – I will be recommending it to all my clients who are, or who manage or support, parental leavers.

Dr Tracey Stead, Co-Lead for Training, Development and Coaching, Future Leaders Fellows Development Network

Contents

Preface

To: Kirstie

From: Graham

Subject: An exciting new project

Kirstie

Will be good to see you back in the office next week. There's an exciting new project that's coming up in Newcastle which I thought would be a great fit for you. I'm catching the train up first thing next Wednesday if you want to book on the same one as me, and then back on Friday evening. That should give you a couple of days back in the office to settle in after your break.

Graham

To: Kirstie

From: Jane

Subject: Welcome back

Hi Kirstie

Hope that you're enjoying your last week of maternity leave and that you're excited about coming back in. I'm in the office on Monday as well so would be good to have a chance to catch up and talk through potential projects that are coming up over the next few months and what's a good fit for you. I've had a chat to Graham and told him to put Cameron on the Newcastle project – there's no way you'll want to be away from home your first week back, or probably your first month back. Look forward to seeing you.

All the best

Jane

When I returned to work after my first maternity leave, I was excited about coming back in, although it was definitely intertwined with a deep sense of uncertainty about how I was going to juggle both roles and get my head back into it after six months of baby talk. I had mixed views about the emails from my two directors. Although it was great that Graham thought I'd be up for the Newcastle

https://doi.org/10.1515/9783111618456-204

project, "hooray they still think my brain works ok", it did feel daunting. Conversely it was very helpful to have that level of empathy and understanding from Jane, but was that because she thought I wasn't up to it?

This book is designed to guide you through this tricky transition back to work whether you're the manager, like Graham and Jane, trying to support in the best way, or if you are the returning parent trying to figure out how to maintain both your career and your role as a mum or dad. This was all more than 20 years ago and the research, coaching and expertise I've built up over the intervening years, and shared in the following pages, will hopefully help you manage this adjustment into working parenthood.

Chapter 1: Introduction

Thanks for picking up this book or starting to read it on your e-reader. Each chapter starts with a summary of what's covered so that you can quickly go to the areas that are most relevant for you. This first chapter provides the context to help you get the most out of reading this book, specifically it covers:

– Who is this book aimed at?
– Why is this important?
– Why have I written this book?
– How is this book structured?
– Types of support.

Who is this book aimed at?

For many people, returning to work after maternity, paternity or adoption leave is one of the biggest life changes they will face. Although you have hopefully experienced great joy upon becoming a parent and have a sense of excitement about returning to work, the transition from being a working professional, to a stay-at-home parent, to then a working parent, can feel like a significant challenge. You may be feeling guilty about leaving your baby, concerned about getting up to speed with changes at work or worried about dealing with expectations and assumptions from others. This book aims to provide practical, evidence-based help for what you can do as a returning parent to support yourself through this transition, with a series of reflective questions to consider, exercises, and thoughts on conversations to have with your line manager.

The return from parental leave is a shared responsibility, so as well as exploring how as a returning parent you can support yourself, this book provides guidance for managers on how to best support those returning from parental leave. As a manager you probably have great intentions when it comes to managing returning parents, however, you may lack the awareness, strategies or time to effectively manage this tricky transition on returning to work. This book provides practical strategies and checklists for you to support parental returners for a smoother transition, whilst the numerous quotes and case studies should provide an increased awareness of the variety of experiences for those returning as working parents.

This book is primarily aimed at working professionals and their managers, those who are looking to manage their career alongside being a parent. If you view your work more as a job rather than a career, there are still lots of techniques

https://doi.org/10.1515/9783111618456-001

and tips within the book that you can put into practice, however, some of the sections on managing your career are likely to be less relevant.

Although this book could have been called "Returning successfully" or "Returning productively" the emphasis is on "Returning *well*" so that in conjunction with managing your career, or as a manager helping your returner manage their career and return successfully, the guidance here is also aimed at managing well-being for working parents. For each stage of the journey for you as a working parent, there are strategies for managing both your career and your well-being, whether that's how to effectively prepare for parental leave, setting up for your return to work, or how to make a successful transition when you are back in the workplace.

Much of the research, case studies and further resources shared throughout this book are UK-based, however, there are numerous examples drawn from other countries and the learnings can be applied if you're a returning parent or supporting manager from a different location. Similarly, although more of the research and experience in this field is connected with those taking maternity leave, families come in all shapes and sizes, so research and guidance is included to take account of the broad range of ways you can return as a working parent, including coming back from adoption leave, or returning after extended paternity leave. Throughout this book it refers to "parental leave" to cover maternity, paternity and adoption leave, unless the research is focused on a specific area.

Why is this important?

Returning to work after taking parental leave is hard – often it can be very hard. As you might expect, research shows that returning to work after maternity leave is challenging, with impacts on well-being for working mothers and increased employee turnover causing difficulties for organisations.[1] Changes and progress are happening, but slowly and we still have a way to go.

The importance of both encouraging and enabling mothers to return to the workforce, and facilitating fathers taking parental leave, has been recognised by successive UK governments with a stream of legislation aimed at increasing the benefits, rights and choices for parents. For example, changes introduced through the Work and Families Act 2006, the Equality Act 2010 and the Children and Families Act 2014 have made it easier for women to both spend more time on maternity leave and to stay in contact whilst off, with the introduction of Keeping in Touch (KIT) days. The ability to take Shared Parental Leave (SPL), in place since April 2015, can give you the flexibility to share up to 50 weeks leave during a baby's first year, providing benefits for both mums and dads. In the UK there has also been a greater focus on flexibility, which has brought benefits for both parents and non-parents, including the right to ask for flexible working from the start of employment.

Organisations are also increasingly recognising the importance of encouraging and keeping mothers in the workforce and developing family-friendly policies and support for both mothers and fathers. These policies and support can help maintain well-being and minimize the financial and disruptive impact of employee turnover.

This may sound like good news and these changes from both government and organisations are having an impact. On the positive side there has been a shift in workplace demographics, with more mothers now in employment. ONS data[2] shows that the employment rate for mothers in 2021 was 76% an increase of 7% since 2013, whilst research[3] suggests that over 80% of UK professional women return to work after maternity leave, taking an average of nine months leave.

However, studies[4] indicate that despite more legislated benefits and workplace policies, progress in supporting maternity returners and working parents is still lacking, we have a way to go. For example, the UK is viewed as offering limited maternity support compared to other European countries, particularly Scandinavia[5], whilst mandatory paid maternity leave doesn't exist in the U.S. the only one of the OECD countries not to do so.

In addition, despite the introduction of Shared Parental Leave (SPL) in the UK, research[6] indicates that only 1–2% of eligible fathers take advantage of this policy and share parental leave during the baby's first year. This research also shows that dads who do take SPL not only face similar challenges to returning mothers, but also additional hurdles such as going against gendered expectations of who takes time off for parental leave, and lacking the same support as returning mothers. So, although this legislation may look like a step in the right direction, in reality it's not having a big impact on reducing the challenges for new working parents.

Why have I written this book?

So, if we recognise the importance of supporting returning parents, what are the benefits of a new book in this area? Although there are a few books looking at how to transition to working parenthood, there have been a lot of recent changes in how we work, both as a result of the legislation mentioned above, but also changes to our working patterns, such as increased homeworking. Previous literature has mainly focused on guidance for returning mothers and doesn't take into consideration the small but growing body of fathers taking shared parental leave; there is also a lack of guidance for the manager or organisation supporting the return to work. This book takes a different angle, considering it a shared responsibility – by understanding where the manager is coming from as well as understanding the returner's position, this book aims to help both manage the successful transition to working parenthood.

When I returned from maternity leave for the first time in 2004, back to my role as an executive coach and consultant, I don't think I fully understood how best to support myself. Although I read widely whilst I was pregnant and on maternity leave, I didn't ever find a book that really helped me think through how to return. I hadn't realised at the time just how supportive my manager Jane was. She showed a deep understanding of the types of challenges I was experiencing and how best to support me. However, during my many years of working as a coach with parental returners and their managers, and also my organisational psychology research with maternity returners[7], I know there can be wide variations in the levels of support from managers. Any lack of managerial support is often through being time-poor or unwittingly not fully understanding the challenges of the return from parental leave. There can also be a real lack of guidance to help managers.

This book is based on my 25+ years of working as a coach and also my organisational psychology research and expertise – aiming to provide practical support backed up by evidence-based research. Returning parents often talk about how it's helpful to realise that they are not alone and to understand the experiences of others who are going through a similar transition to a professional working parent. Dotted throughout this book are quotes from returning parents I've worked with, interviewed or who are professional colleagues of mine, to help understand the range of experiences returning parents go through. As a manager or HR leader understanding the experiences of those that are about to go or return from parental leave can also help you to offer the best support at each of these transition points.

Several of my colleagues within my coaching network have asked me why I'm effectively giving away my trade secrets, sharing the research, tools and techniques that would naturally be covered during 1:1 and group coaching for returners and their managers. Although that is a potential risk, particularly as I have designed this book to be as comprehensive as possible, I figure there will still be a need for some returners and managers to have that in-person coaching support, with this book being a guide for those I coach.

Also, and more importantly, many individuals won't be fortunate enough to work for organisations where coaching is a possibility and therefore hopefully for either you as the manager or as a working parent, you can use this guide together to help navigate through leaving and returning from parental leave. I sincerely hope through sharing my research and coaching experience this book helps guide you through what is an exciting but challenging transition.

How is this book structured?

Some of us are natural pickers, dipping into the parts that interest us or we have time to delve into, rather than reading books from cover to cover. This book has been set up to allow you to do that, with the next three chapters following a natural flow from preparing to leave (Chapter 2), setting up for return (Chapter 3) and the initial return from parental leave (Chapter 4). This allows you as a manager or returning parent to focus on the stage you are currently at.

Each of these three chapters has been structured to firstly consider the changes, challenges and experiences at that stage of the parental journey. The second part of Chapters 2, 3 and 4 is focused on the leaver/returner's perspective, giving some practical strategies to think through at that stage, whether that's leaving, preparing for return, or the initial return.

Thirdly, for each of these chapters there is a section focused on the manager's perspective. This is based on experiences of other managers and leaders who have supported those going through this transition and provides guidance and practical advice on how to support those leaving and returning from parental leave.

Finally, for those that naturally go for the summary version there is a checklist at the end of each chapter highlighting the key areas to focus on.

The majority of this book is aimed at either the returner themselves or their manager, however, Chapter 5 is also geared at those within the broader organisation, such as HR or People teams, sharing how they can best support both returning parents and their managers.

The final chapter considers the experiences and support for returners after they have been back for a few months, adjusting to a new identity and patterns of working parenthood. This includes guidance on managing working patterns which is applicable to anyone who feels under pressure and/or has commitments outside the workplace and includes a focus on homeworking which is becoming increasingly common post Covid-19.

Types of support

Support for those returning to the workplace exists at five different levels, as shown in the following illustration. At the macro level there is *National* support from government and society through to the support that the returners give themselves, their *Self-support*. Throughout this book we will look at how both managers and returners can tap into these different levels of support, whether that's how to maximise the use of national benefits, understanding and using company policies, or utilising support from the returner's team.

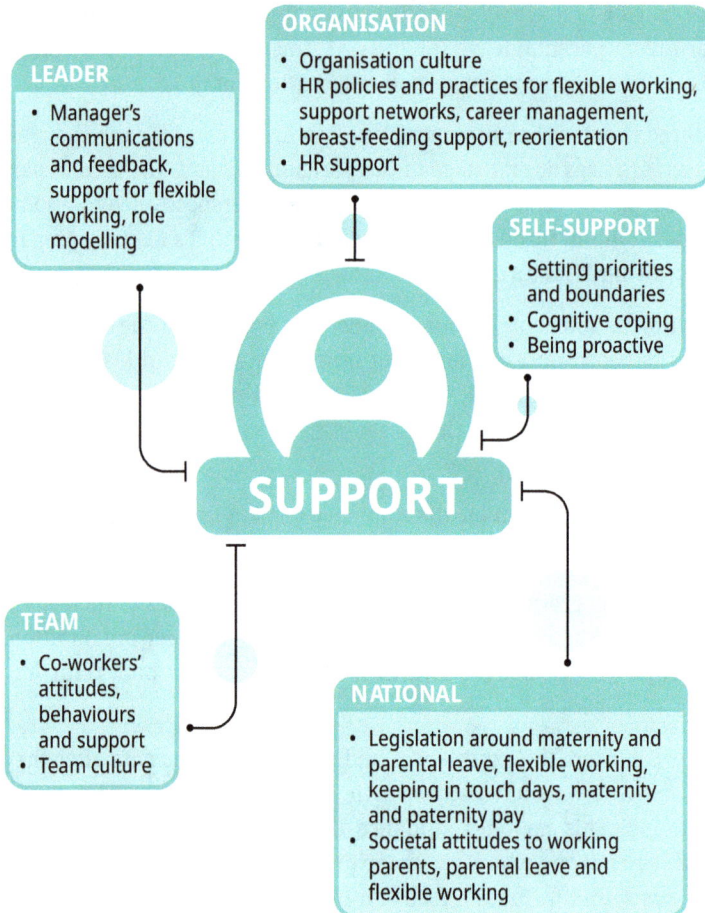

LEADER
- Manager's communications and feedback, support for flexible working, role modelling

ORGANISATION
- Organisation culture
- HR policies and practices for flexible working, support networks, career management, breast-feeding support, reorientation
- HR support

SELF-SUPPORT
- Setting priorities and boundaries
- Cognitive coping
- Being proactive

SUPPORT

TEAM
- Co-workers' attitudes, behaviours and support
- Team culture

NATIONAL
- Legislation around maternity and parental leave, flexible working, keeping in touch days, maternity and paternity pay
- Societal attitudes to working parents, parental leave and flexible working

Figure 1: Types of support.

Chapter 2: Setting up to leave

Although the focus of this book is how to return well, there are a number of areas that soon-to-be parents, and their managers, can consider *before* going off on leave, to help the return go as smoothly as possible. This chapter explores:

– Understanding the changes – understanding the experiences and emotions of those about to go on leave and tackling concerns.
– The leaver's perspective – how to leave well through managing your cover, career and communications to set up for the best return.
– The manager's perspective – understanding typical concerns and offering support.
– Checklist – summary actions for leaving parents and their managers.

Understanding the changes

When going through a period of change, there can be sense of moving out of your comfort zone, leaving familiar territory and stepping into the unknown. Becoming a parent is one of the most significant life changes you can undergo and in the months leading up to a maternity, paternity or adoption leave there can be a range of emotions that soon-to-be parents typically experience. These can vary from feeling guilty about leaving others to pick up your work, excitement about the upcoming new baby, feeling left out as you are progressively not included in work decisions, to uncertainty as it all feels so new.

In addition, if you're the mother, you may be coping with pregnancy symptoms which make it harder to work at your usual capacity all the time and others may be treating you differently or saying things that feel annoying or upsetting.

> *"People keep touching my bump or making comments about my size which makes me feel very uncomfortable."*

> *"I've lost track of how many people have told me that I need to enjoy a good night's sleep while I can – it's really irritating."*

Coping with a range of emotions, being treated differently, and experiencing physical changes often means that parents don't dedicate time for setting themselves up in the right way for returning to work. Taking the time to put into place practical steps and reflecting on where you are emotionally can pay huge dividends in helping you leave in a way that sets you up for the best possible return, which is the aim of this chapter.

https://doi.org/10.1515/9783111618456-002

When going off on parental leave, there is a transition from being a working professional to a stay-at-home mum or dad. This change hopefully brings lots of joy and excitement, but often throws up concerns as well. For some people there may be apprehension about what might be ending, whilst others may worry about what new things are going to be in their lives that they're unsure about. There may also be practical concerns about money, worries about how being a parent will change your relationship with your partner, or concerns about leaving work.

At the root of many concerns is a sense of the unknown and the potential the human brain can have to catastrophise, imagining the worst-case scenario.

> *"I'm really worried that lots of the things I take for granted I'm not going to be able to do anymore, such as spontaneously going out, spending time with my partner or having lie-ins."*

What can be helpful is to articulate and write down what those concerns are and then do a reality check on how true they really are, rather than letting your brain potentially go into what's known as "catastrophise mode."

To help make this reflection on concerns practical, you can think through the actions that you can put in place to address each of these concerns. A helpful way to structure this is to think through what you are expecting to end, what you are expecting to be new and then doing a reality check and action list. Examples of these steps are shown in the table below:

Table 1: Reality check.

	Concern	Reality check	Action
What am I expecting to end?	*Not being able to spontaneously go out.*	*The same level of spontaneity will be tricky, but babies are portable, or I can organise a sitter.*	*Determine who I have in my support network to step-in and/or sitters I can use.*
What am I expecting to be new?	*I've heard lots of horror stories about sleepless nights.*	*I'm probably more likely to hear about those that have challenges rather than those whose babies sleep ok.*	*If I do end up with a more restless baby, then allow myself to have naps during the day. Also talk to others about strategies for helping babies sleep.*
What else am I concerned about?			

If you find it tricky to do this reality check, then it's useful to talk through your concerns with a friend or partner, if you have one, asking them to gently challenge and help you reframe, so that you can articulate an alternative reality.

> *"I really worried I would struggle to go back to work and still be taken seriously, my partner helped me realise I was probably worrying unnecessarily and got me to think through how likely that really was."*

It can also help to reflect on what is actually staying the same, rather than falling into the trap of worrying that everything is going to be different. Because going on parental leave and having a baby can feel like such a momentous change, your brain sometimes focuses on all the things that are changing, rather than recognising that lots will be the same, whether that's your job, your home or your relationships with friends and family. Hopefully most of these things will be constant, which can act as a stabiliser while other parts of your life are changing, and if possible, avoid significant changes such as moving house whilst you're going through this period of transition.

Identity changes when you're pregnant

Research[8] shows that a mother's ability to manage the shift in their identities when they become pregnant is one of the most significant challenges they experience. As well as their existing identity of being a working professional and having a career, they now also have a transitory identity as someone who is pregnant. These identities can be in conflict with each other particularly as pregnancy can be associated with negative stereotypes (see later in this chapter for how to manage stereotypes). I've seen many times in my coaching the shift that can happen, with a loss of confidence and sense of self when women become pregnant.

This can be exacerbated by the emerging sense of identity of becoming a mother with a lack of clarity on what this new motherhood identity will look like, and how that will be compatible with their existing identity of being a working professional.

Giving yourself time to accept any sense of loss, focusing on activities that help boost your sense of well-being and developing a vision of the kind of working parent you want to be, can all help you manage this identity change. The research shows that successfully navigating this transition increases levels of engagement, commitment and satisfaction.

One of the recommendations I often give those deciding when to go off on parental leave, is to leave one or two weeks before the due date to allow for the transition of being out of the workplace and at home before their baby is born. This allows the acceptance and adjustment to loss of work and its associated status to start to embed before the next identity transition of being a new parent.

As well as practically taking things easier if you are the mum and at that large and uncomfortable stage of your last few weeks of pregnancy, taking time off allows for a smoother transition to home life before the baby is born. Getting your head around no longer being at work and having that professional identity, potential status and fulfilment of work, before adjusting to the identity of being a parent.

> *"I was a bit sceptical about taking off time before my baby was born as I thought it would be better to save as much of my maternity leave as possible for when the baby was here, but I'm so glad I took your advice. I hadn't realised what an adjustment it would be just being at home and not having the buzz of going into the office."*

The leaver's perspective

One of the first questions you are likely to be asking yourself is how long you want to take off for parental leave. Clearly this is a very personal decision and will depend on your financial circumstances, what paid and unpaid leave is available to you (depending on your organisation and geography) and also what feels right for you and your partner, if you have one. It's worth recognising that you may be feeling under pressure to decide in a certain way based on expectations from others, if so it's helpful to take a step back and think about what feels the right decision for you and your family, rather than succumbing to those external or societal pressures. There are more details on rationalising decisions in the section *Cognitive coping* within *Chapter 4: The initial return.*

As part of your decision making about taking leave, it's worth challenging any assumptions you've made around what's feasible as the below example illustrates:

> *"My organization is really good as it offers four months paternity leave, which is pretty generous in the U.S. When I was considering leave, I asked them if instead of four months it was possible to take eight months but working half my hours. Although that had never been done before they were very open to it and it's been great as it's allowed me to keep working with my clients, stay in touch with my team, while spending that important time bonding with our son. It's also meant that my wife has been able to work flexibly which has been wonderful for her."*

Although some people may have had sabbaticals or extended time off, for most parents, before they go off on maternity, paternity or adoption leave the maximum time they would have been out of the workplace will have been a couple of weeks of annual holiday, and even then they may still be checking emails. The average length of maternity leave in the UK is nine months[9] and being out for this significant period can be a big adjustment.

Even if as a returning mother or father you only take a few months out of the workplace, with the average maternity leave in the U.S. being 10 weeks,[10] it is still worth thinking through how to leave well to set up for the best return. Aside from thinking through how much parental leave to take, the three areas to focus on before you take parental leave are: who is going to cover my work whilst I'm off, how do I manage my career and what communications need to be in place.

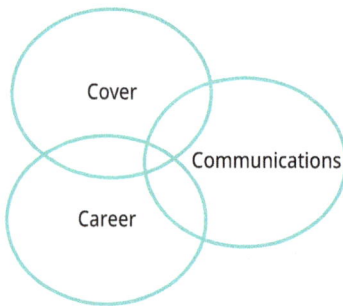

Figure 2: Focus areas for leaving well – the 3 Cs.

Cover

Depending on how long your leave is, there are a number of questions to think through on how your work and responsibilities are going to be managed whilst you're away:

- What feasibly can I finish before I go off on leave?
- What work could be put on hold or hibernated, that I could pick up again when I'm back?
- If I can't finish or hibernate work, what projects or responsibilities do I need to hand-over before I go off?
- If I have a team or people reporting to me, what do I need to put in place before I go off to make sure they are set up for my absence and have support whilst I'm away?
- Who within the current team / department / organisation could take my work on?
- If there isn't anyone to pick up my work, or all of my work, what cover do I need to organise for when I'm away?

When planning out how your work will be covered, it is helpful to not commit to deadlines in the last two weeks before you leave. Although babies, particularly first ones, are more likely to arrive late, things may not go to plan. If you do end up with a parental leave cover, allowing a couple of weeks overlap enables you to hand over responsibilities, whilst still being there to answer any questions, rather than being called upon whilst you're off.

"I was happily wandering around the store's baby department in my final days of pregnancy when I got a call through from my Director – it was a real pain

to have to drag myself back into work mode and help him think through the details of a project."

Additionally, allowing for a period of overlap, if possible, will also enable you to build a relationship with your parental cover to ensure a smooth handover and help you feel more confident about letting go. Whilst sorting out the logistics of handing your work over can be tricky, what many parents to be find harder is emotionally letting go of their work. Typically, the concerns people have around parental leave cover include:

–   What if they do a better job than me?
–   What if people prefer them to me?
–   What if they muck up the projects or plans that I have put in place?
–   What if this new person highlights all the things I've been doing wrong?

"I did the interviews for my maternity cover and ended up choosing someone who I thought would be similar, but not quite as good as me – I didn't want to get shown up."

"I have a really important project I've been working on, and I really don't want to hand it over as I'm worried all of my hard work will get lost, they will mess it up or I won't get credit for it."

These are really natural reactions to having parental leave cover, and you're certainly not alone if you are feeling any of these concerns. Getting involved in the process of deciding who is going to cover your work, if this is feasible, can partly alleviate these concerns. However, it's helpful to recognise that you have limited control or influence on how your parental cover performs or is liked. What you do have control over though, is how you manage your own career and how you connect in and communicate with others in a way that sets you up for the best possible return.

The trick is to try and focus on the things that you can control or influence rather than spending time on areas that you are concerned about, but actually can't do anything about. The adage used in the competitive sports world is "control the controllables". One way of thinking about this is viewing your concerns as a layer or cover around you, which acts almost as a suffocating blanket and reduces your ability to think clearly. When you focus too much on your concerns, it makes this layer around you heavier and thicker reducing your ability to focus on what you can control or influence.

You can think about your ability to control or influence as seedlings that are trying to break through this layer of concern. If the concern is too thick and heavy it makes it hard for the seedlings to break through. Whereas instead, if you focus on the seedlings, those things you can control and influence, in effect you're making them become stronger so they can break through the concern layer.

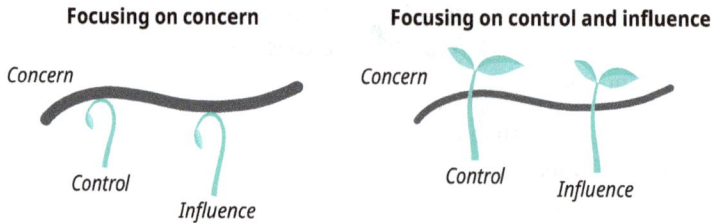

Focusing on concern   **Focusing on control and influence**

Concern   *Concern*

Control   *Control*   *Influence*

Influence

Figure 3: Focus on what you can control and influence.

For example, you may be concerned about your maternity cover. You can't control who your maternity cover is going to be, but by getting involved in the recruitment process you can influence the decision. What we can control is our mindset or how we view the situation, recognising that it can be helpful to reframe.

Career management

When heading off on an extended period of leave in connection with your new baby, often the last thing on your mind can be considerations around your career. However, if you want to return in the best possible way, it's useful to spend some time thinking through how you stabilise or build your career and maintain your visibility. There are three main areas to consider: appraisal and promotion discussions, career opportunities on return, leaving on a high.

Depending on how your leave coincides with key points in your company's annual review cycle, it's important to speak to your manager and/or HR to complete any performance reviews before you leave and to make sure that you're being included in any appraisal discussions whilst you're away, including promotion discussions if that's right for you.

> *"I was already feeling guilty about leaving, so didn't feel I could also have discussions about my promotion."*

> *"I'm worried that I'm going to get forgotten whilst I'm away and miss out."*

How you are appraised for the performance year whilst you are off on parental leave should be based on your performance during the time you are at work, and not in comparison to achievement levels of others who have worked a whole year. However, to help ensure this happens it's important to have discussions before you go off, as you won't be there to participate in any reviews whilst you are on leave.

It may be that your organisation doesn't have formal review cycles or appraisals, however, it's still worth having discussions with your manager before you leave to review where you are. Additionally, whatever the type of performance management in your organisation, setting yourself up with allies, both officially and unofficially, can be a great way to help manage your career in the right direction.

> *"I knew my manager wouldn't be particularly supportive in helping me think through my career options, so I made sure that I had conversations with others in the organisation whom I knew understood the experience of going off on maternity leave."*

The second career area to focus on is thinking about your role on return. Although it may be that you want to return to the same role, with the same working pattern (e.g. full or part-time), depending on the opportunities within your organisation, it's worth considering what other potential roles you would like. Without committing yourself, having conversations before you go with your manager and other potential mentors can help you be front of mind if opportunities that you'd like to be considered for come up whilst you're off.

> *"I'm planning on having catch-ups with managers in other departments so they can help me think about what roles I could go for when I return."*

The final area to consider is "leaving on a high." Although you probably don't want to put additional pressure on yourself before going off on leave, if your career is important to you, spending time thinking about how you make yourself visible, ensuring your contributions are recognised and valued, can help you leave with a strong positive impression. This isn't around struggling to take on extra responsibilities or additional challenges, but more thinking about how you can position yourself so that you stay memorable, for the right reasons, whilst you're away.

Balanced with leaving on a high, it's worth considering the expectations you have of yourself in the last few months before going off. Particularly if you are pregnant, rather than a non-pregnant partner or going on adoption leave, the changes your body is going through may mean you need to adjust your working patterns where possible, for example cutting down on travel and making the most of hybrid working.

"We had a first-aid room, where you could take a nap during the day if you needed it. I felt really guilty for using it, but then realised it helped me work better for the rest of the day and at that late stage of pregnancy I had to listen to what my body needed."

Should I be "leaning in"?

Sheryl Sandberg's widely read book, **Lean in**[11] has been an international best seller, with over two million copies sold since its publication in 2013, spawning over 43,000 Lean in circles,[12] or support groups, in 170+ different countries. The book advocates that instead of inadvertently holding themselves back, women should "lean in", change their mind-sets and step up to leadership roles.

My experience working with those going on maternity leave shows that some identify strongly with the themes highlighted throughout the book and find it a useful self-help guide, whilst others feel it puts additional pressure on themselves and doesn't feel right for them at this time.

"It's really important to me that I get considered for the promotion whilst I'm on mat leave, so I really need to think about how to make myself visible."

"After a lot of soul searching, I decided to accept the new role when I came back, as although it was a sideways move, it allowed me to feel I was doing the best by my daughter."

A balanced perspective is provided by a great review in Academy of Management Perspectives.[13] This paper provides an evidence-based critique of the book, examining which of the arguments within the book are supported by research and which are more popular management hype. For example, there is limited evidence to show that women may be holding themselves back, whilst there is evidence around the assumptions others make about working mothers. The book describes how assumptions from others, that working mothers don't want to pursue their career in the same way, can act as a barrier and hold women back.

In analysing why the book has been so popular, the authors reach the conclusion that those that are reading it are already achievement-orientated and so the advice fits with their current career aspirations and point of view. A classic example of confirmation bias where we seek out evidence that matches our current viewpoint.

My experience working with maternity returners, is that rather than asking "But shouldn't I be leaning in?", the more helpful question to ask is "Do I want to lean in?".

Communications

There are two areas within communications it is useful to focus on when preparing to go on parental leave, firstly, who do you need to be in contact with before you leave and secondly, what type of communication do you want to have whilst off on leave. As already highlighted, before you go on parental leave, there are useful conversations to have with your manager about how your responsibilities will be covered and how to stabilise your career. Other people you need to communicate with are the various colleagues, stakeholders and clients you have, letting them know your plans for when you're leaving and how your work is going to be picked up.

Secondly, before you leave it's helpful to agree with your manager and others, what type of contact you want whilst you are off, to reduce uncertainty and avoid confusion. If you have never taken an extended period off before, it can be hard to get your head around not being in regular contact with the organisation, particularly if you're someone who finds it hard to switch off and not check emails whilst on holidays. For example, a client of mine before going off on parental leave talked about how *"I assume I'm still going to be logging on whilst I'm off, I can't imagine not being in contact."* However, when speaking to them whilst they were off on parental leave they had a quite different response: *"The office now feels a million miles away, I really feel disconnected and although it was great to go in and show them our baby, I really don't want to know what's going on day to day."*

The recommendation is to take yourself off distribution lists and updates whilst you're away so that emails don't pile up. Although the advice would be to not plan on checking your emails, it is useful to agree how you'll be kept updated for any significant changes that happen whilst you're away. What you see as significant will be a personal choice, but whilst you're off with your little one, you're less likely to be worried about updates on a project, whereas a significant organisation change you may want to be kept up to date with. What those on leave often find most helpful is to be sent a text or email to their personal email address, so that they don't get sucked back into their work email. There is more in the next chapter about staying in contact whilst off on leave.

The manager's perspective

So far, this chapter has considered the perspective of the parent who is about to go off on maternity, paternity or adoption leave, helping them think through how they leave to set themselves up for the best return. As a manager it's helpful to read this first part to understand where your prospective parent may be coming from, particularly if you are not a parent yourself or it's been a while since you were returning from parental leave. The next part of this chapter considers things from the manager's perspective, understanding the typical concerns managers can experience and how they can best support their leaving parent, recognising the shared responsibility.

Although this next section is aimed at managers, if you are the prospective parent, it can be helpful to read this to understand the other viewpoint and potentially nudge this section in your manager's direction.

Typical manager concerns

Those who are managing leavers can often feel worried that they may say the wrong thing, either from a legal perspective or from a personal and emotional perspective.

> *"I've avoided having conversations with my maternity leaver because I'm worried I'm going to put my foot in it."*

Additionally, depending on how long the leaver is absent for, there may be concerns about how the work is going to be covered whilst the person is away.

> *"Although I was pleased for them about their upcoming baby, inwardly I was worried that they may not come back and how I was going to cover their role whilst they're off."*

> *"I'd never say this out loud, but my initial reaction was 'damn how is that project going to be covered'."*

For those managing employees going off on adoption leave there may also be concerns around the level of uncertainty on when the employee is going to start their leave.

Although these are all common concerns, it's important to avoid leaking any of these thoughts to your parental leaver.

"When I told my manager I was pregnant [for a second time], his immediate response was 'oh I thought you'd finished with all that'."

Another potential area of concern for managers is understanding the current policies and legal situation – hopefully you can get guidance from any HR support you have. As extra resources, for those managing maternity, paternity or adoption leavers in UK, the ACAS website gives comprehensive details on regulations around leave (https://www.acas.org.uk/maternity-paternity-and-adoption-leave-and-pay), whilst in the U.S. Paycor offer guidance on parental leave by state (https://www.paycor.com/resource-center/articles/maternity-leave-laws-by-state/).

Managing adoption leave

The process of managing parents going off on adoption leave can present extra challenges due to the levels of uncertainty, as exemplified by the thoughts below from a team manager who works in academia.

"Although I think it's great that my team member has been accepted to be a potential adoptive parent, I've got to be honest it makes life really tricky for us and the department. The adoption process seems to be fairly last minute, the first time we only found out they were successful and therefore going to go off on adoption leave a few weeks before it was due to happen, and then at the last minute the process fell through and so they naturally then wanted to cancel their adoption leave. I really felt for them as I'm sure they were incredibly disappointed, but we're now going through the process again with that level of uncertainty about when they are going to go off. It means that I don't want to put them onto any long-term projects and it's hard to involve them in future planning as we don't know if they're going to be around or not. It really isn't their fault, and there isn't anything they should be doing differently, but it doesn't stop it being very tricky."

To help cope with this as a manager it's clearly important to have regular conversation with your potential adopting parent so that you can be kept informed, but it can also be helpful to practise a level of acceptance, recognising that it's a tricky situation which you have a limited ability to control. (There are more details on practicing acceptance as part of *Cognitive coping* in Chapter 4.)

Offering support

As a manager, supporting your leaver in setting up their parental cover, stabilising their career and maintaining communications helps ensure they'll come back and also that the work gets covered whilst they're away.

For support connected to parental cover it's helpful to keep the parental leaver involved, recognising any concerns they may have. It's useful to start the process three to four months before they are due to go on leave, particularly if you are looking to recruit someone to take over the role in their absence rather than the work being covered by existing members of the team. Starting the recruitment process early can help alleviate any potential additional concerns.

> *"I'm due to go off on maternity leave next month and I still don't have any cover in place which is adding extra stress that I really don't need."*

It's recommended that you talk through any final handover plans in the two to four weeks before leave, to ensure the work and responsibilities are either being covered or put on hold, whilst the employee is away. (There are more details about the different questions to ask on ways to cover the work earlier in this chapter).

From a career's perspective, it's helpful to have any career discussions three to six weeks before leave commences, also making sure that paperwork is completed. Finally, two to four weeks before leaving is a good time to talk through with your parental leaver what level of contact they want whilst they're off and how they want to be kept in touch.

As well as providing practical support around cover, career and communications, offering emotional support is important before, during and after parental leave. Clearly there will be great variation in the type and level of emotional support that your parental leaver is looking for and you hopefully already know the individuals in your team well. However, managers are often surprised at the levels of insecurity, guilt, uncertainty and lack of confidence that individuals feel before going off on parental leave.

> *"I only found out after they left that they were really concerned about going off on maternity leave; I hadn't realised how guilty they felt for leaving their projects for their team-mates to pick up."*

Having regular open and honest conversations with your parental leaver about any concerns they have and how they are feeling will help you understand how to support them in the best way.

However well-intentioned you are, there may also be things that you say or do that may be misinterpreted.

> *"My boss told me they thought the person I recruited as a cover is really great and they may keep them on afterwards. I know she meant well, but that's got me really worried about my own role and concerned that they thought I wasn't good enough."*

> *"My manager has given me lots of advice on how to manage my maternity leave and childcare – he believes he's being helpful, but it just makes me feel that he doesn't have confidence in me."*

The intention you have for your comments or actions may not always land or have the impact you were expecting.

Figure 4: Intention vs impact.

Picking up on the verbal and non-verbal signals from your leaver can help reduce or counteract any potential misinterpretations. For example, how do they react when you make a suggestion or pass on information – are they enthusiastic or do they seem hesitant?

Finally, when providing support it's helpful to think more broadly around any cultural challenges or stereotypes your parental leaver may be experiencing and to tackle these within your team. Whether that's stereotypes associated with being pregnant (more details below), or the potential cultural challenges for fathers choosing to take Shared Parental Leave (more details in the next chapter).

Managing pregnancy stereotypes

Recent research[14] with almost 600 non-pregnant participants, confirmed previous studies showing how when females become pregnant, a set of stereotypes comes into play, with pregnant females being perceived as having lower competence or "baby brain" compared to other groups. Other stereotypes include beliefs that pregnant women don't take work as seriously or are slacking off.

Mothers-to-be recognise these potential stereotypes with studies of pregnant women across a variety of different industries and managerial levels,[15] detailing experiences of how pregnancy can have a negative influence on their professional image in the workplace and how others view them differently, even if they themselves feel the same.

In order to overcome these stereotypes, there are a variety of strategies that pregnant women adopt. Mothers-to-be can go to great lengths to maintain their professional image, including taking on extra work, making sure they operate at the same pace, avoiding asking for any allowances and taking shorter maternity leave.

> *"I know there is a first aid room I've been told I can use if I'm feeling exhausted but there's no way I'd use it as I'd be worried what people think about me."*

> *"I'm really conscious of delivering at the same level I always have as I don't want my manager or team to view me differently."*

Although putting in this extra effort can help pregnant women feel better about themselves, it can be done at a risk to personal health, such as examples in the research where women were concerned about pushing themselves too hard or ignoring doctor's orders to reduce hours with high-risk pregnancies.

Other strategies mothers-to-be adopted to avoid discrimination included hiding or downplaying their pregnancy. Although most pregnant women keep news of their pregnancy private for the first trimester (due to risk of miscarriage), in these studies almost a third hide their pregnancy for longer to avoid negative stereotypes, and others downplayed their pregnancy to avoid drawing attention to it. Adopting these types of strategies places an additional burden on pregnant women with a mismatch between the natural pleasure they may feel about being pregnant and having to pretend it isn't important. This dissonance has been shown to cause stress, anxiety and burnout.

> *"I'm definitely going to delay telling him [my manager] about my pregnancy, as I'm really not sure how he's going to take it."*

This research highlights the important role for both the organisation and the manger in addressing the stereotypes that can occur for pregnant women and helping alleviate pregnant women's concerns about how they are now viewed differently by others. As well as resulting in better well-being outcomes for the women, addressing these stereotypes can reduce the risk of negative outcomes for the organisation such as the risk of discrimination charges, reduced productivity due to burnout and increased employee turnover.

Parental leave checklist

This list is a summary of things to consider either as a leaving parent, or as manager to work through with your leaver.

Checklist	√
Have we identified what projects and responsibilities need to be covered during parental leave and who is going to cover them?	
Has a handover plan and any handover notes been developed?	
Has a performance appraisal been conducted, along with any career development discussions?	
Have stakeholders and colleagues been notified of handover and leaving plans?	
As a leaver, have I thought about potential mentors and connected in with them for career opportunities?	
Have we agreed the types and level of communication whilst on leave?	
As a manager have I counteracted any pregnancy stereotypes or cultural challenges for fathers?	

Chapter 3: Setting up for return

As well as continuing to enjoy parental leave, before coming back to the workplace there are a number of areas to think through to help set up for the best return. This chapter covers:

–   Understanding the challenges – what makes it trickier for returning parents.
–   The returner's perspective – strategies to help with return: getting practicalities sorted, handling common emotions, keeping in contact, choosing how to return.
–   The manager's perspective – strategies for managers: communications, setting up flexible working, career planning, sorting practical aspects, empathy and advice.
–   Returning with additional challenges – coping with postnatal depression, babies with severe illnesses, still births, and how to support as a manager.
–   Checklist – summary actions for preparing to return for parents and their managers.

Understanding the challenges

As you progress through your parental leave, your thoughts may start to turn towards work again, whether that's connecting in with people through KIT days, meeting up socially with work pals, or starting to talk more about work with your partner. To help you be prepared for the return, either as the returning parent or their manager, it's helpful to understand the typical challenges that parental returners face. Although the following section may feel a bit daunting, forewarned is forearmed, and the rest of the chapter looks at strategies for tackling these challenges before the parent returns to work. The following chapter, *Chapter 4: The initial return*, also looks at how you can manage these challenges, as either the returner or as the manager, once the returning parent is back in the workplace.

Based on extensive research with a cross-section of parental returners, and also from listening to parents during my coaching sessions, there are three main categories of challenges that parental returners typically face; thankfully most people don't experience all of them, or not all at once.

https://doi.org/10.1515/9783111618456-003

Out of the loop	Managing a dual role	Culture and norms
Getting up to speed	Adopting multiple identities	Expectations & assumptions from others
Reduced confidence	Guilt	Always - on & presenteeism
Missed career opportunities	Feeling overwhelmed	Male - dominated environments
	Breastfeeding challenges	

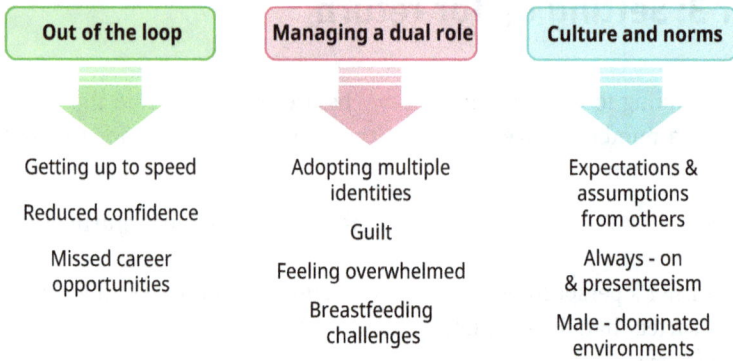

Figure 5: Categories of challenges.

Out of the loop challenges

Being out of the workplace for a chunk of time throws up a number of challenges when you re-enter. Parents often talk about the challenges of getting up to speed with the variety of things that have changed, whether you've been on leave for only a few months or a much longer period. This can vary from staff changes, new systems, new organisational structures, different processes to follow, or new clients that your organisation is working with. When you're in the workplace these adjustments happen gradually, whereas if you've been out for several months, you can be hit with these changes all at once.

> *"I think I underestimated how much I would have missed. So, when I came back, loads of stuff had changed and I hadn't anticipated how much that would throw me."*

> *"When I first came back, I had an awful lot of catching up to do with all the things that had changed in the organisation. I didn't have any real grace period, to take allowance of the catching up I needed to do, so I struggled."*

Depending on your profession there may also be changes in standards, legislation, guidance or current practice that you need to get up to date with.

> *"A lot of the guidance had changed whilst I was away, so I found I was having to look things up much more or ask my boss, which didn't make me feel great."*

Parents are often surprised about the amount of time it takes to adjust back, with returners feeling that it can take three, four, or up to six months to feel like they've fully adjusted back to the workplace, getting up to speed and managing the dual roles of parent and professional. Recognising that as a returning parent it's normal to have this period of adjustment can help reduce the levels of stress associated with getting up to speed. Additionally as a manager, or team member of a returning parent, some recognition of this challenge is helpful.

Feeling out of the loop can also have an impact on confidence when you return to the workplace, which can also be exacerbated if you have had a maternity or paternity cover doing your role whilst you were away.

> *"Understanding what my new role was, combined with everything being new, and getting my brain back into gear. Um, it's probably fair to say I lost a bit of confidence."*

> *"I really struggled with what a good job my maternity cover seemed to have done whilst I was off, which knocked my sense of belief in myself, and I wondered whether they should be doing the role instead of me."*

A final challenge within this category is feeling that you have missed out on career opportunities. There may have been organisational changes or promotion rounds whilst you were off and depending on your levels of contact whilst away and how you've connected in before you left, you may be feeling that you've missed out. There may also have been restructures and/or redundancy programs which may impact your career options.

> *"What frustrates me the most is that I missed out on being able to put my hand up for a new role, because all of that [organisation restructure] was done in a vacuum and I wasn't here to fight my corner."*

Although these out of the loop challenges may feel daunting, there are a variety of ways to tackle these, which are picked up later in this chapter.

Managing the challenges of a dual role

There are a number of challenges associated with managing the dual role of being both a parent and a working professional, the first of which is connected with adopting multiple identities. Prior to having children there are many different roles or identities you can have in life whether that's being a partner, a working professional, a friend, a carer, a sporting person, or numerous other identities. Although at times combining these different identities can be challenging, for many the transition to adopting the identities of being both a parent and a working professional can feel one of the hardest and where there is the greatest likelihood of conflict.

> *"I'm going home now and going to be in mum mode for a day, and then I'm back into work the following day. . . . It's like flicking a switch, which I find very, very hard."*

> *"The first time my child was ill was when it really hit me around the challenges of juggling both roles – it was literally the day of my first big client presentation since I'd gone back into work, and I had a call a couple of hours after I'd got into the office saying my child was ill and I needed to pick them up. At first, I thought 'well I can't because I need to do this presentation' and then I realised I didn't have a choice and had to leave the office – I was gutted."*

Becoming a parent can feel like a big identity change and there are often struggles parents feel about how they adopt the role of both parent and professional in a way that feels comfortable and authentic for them.

This sense of adopting dual identities and combining the commitments involved in both work and being a parent can often lead to experiences of guilt.

> *"I feel guilty that I just can't do everything. I don't feel like I can do anything well. I'm not doing my job well and I'm not being a great parent or a great partner. And I feel guilty when I get home that I've not finished everything in work and that I should probably log on in the evenings."*

This sense of guilt can be exacerbated by societal norms around what it means to be a good parent. If as a parent you feel that you're not living up to, or conforming to, norms around "good parenting" then it can trigger or increase your sense of guilt.

Research[16] shows this is particularly acute for mothers who are working through choice rather than financial necessity. If as a mother you are working because you want to, whether that's because you find it fulfilling, challenging, enjoyable or part of your identity, then you are more likely to feel a sense of guilt than if you are working because you feel that financially you have no choice. Gender stereotypes have been shown to result in perceptions of mothers who choose to work as "bad parents", less committed to their families and also less warm and caring. These perceptions from others can increase the sense of guilt that working mothers feel.

As well as experiencing guilt, another challenge associated with managing the dual role of being both a parent and a professional is a sense of feeling overwhelmed. Trying to juggle everything, particularly when first returning to work, can leave returning parents struggling:

> *"I'm struggling to manage my working days so that I can get out the door at a decent time because I know the nursery will shut. And old me would have just worked at the weekend or sat there until late at night and blitzed it, but new me doesn't have the opportunity to do that. It's a constant juggling act."*

Strategies for how you deal with these potential challenges of managing multiple identities, guilt and feeling overwhelmed are picked up in the rest of this chapter and also in more detail in *Setting boundaries and priorities* in the next chapter.

A final dual role challenge is for mothers who are aiming to maintain breastfeeding when returning to work. Although many organisations have started to put in place facilities for mothers who want to express whilst at work, there are many cases where mothers are having to hide in the toilets or their cars to use their breast pump. Even if facilities are in place there can still be difficulties with accessing the room, lack of locks on the door, nowhere to store milk and other challenges.

> *"I pumped at work which was tricky. It was hard . . . it was really hard."*

Tied in with this can be concerns about finding the time to be able to express and being seen as slacking for not being at your work space.

> *"My days were so busy when I returned, I struggled to find the time to be able to express, and even when I did, I felt bad about it."*

Finding out about available facilities, thinking through the logistics and chatting to others who've had experience of continuing to breastfeed on their return to work can help ease your concerns and make managing breastfeeding easier.

> *"Before I went back to work, I found out how others had managed it, and I also bought one of those fancy breast pumps that's very discreet so that I could pump my milk whilst still staying at my desk – that made a huge difference."*

Adopting these strategies can then help avoid having to cease breastfeeding earlier than you want to.

"I ended up getting myself really upset because I had to stop breastfeeding much earlier than I wanted to, I just couldn't manage pumping at work."

These strategies, of thinking through how you can feasibly continue breastfeeding when back at work are if you are the returning birth mother. If instead you are the manager or part of HR, there is also guidance on setting up breastfeeding support as part of *Organisation initiatives* in *Chapter 5: Support from HR and the broader organisation*.

Culture and norms challenges

The final set of challenges is connected with the culture of the organisation and the teams you work in, and also societal norms around working parents. There can be expectations and assumptions about your commitment, career aspirations, priorities and ability to manage.

"Everyone's perception is it's probably easy to have one baby and work. I felt I had to live up to that."

"I think part of their decision for not giving me the new role was that I'm on a mommy track now. I've heard of that assumption through a lot of other people and their experiences."

There may also be societal norms and expectations that put an additional level of challenge on you.

"I'm definitely finding it challenging with my in-laws as they keep dropping not so subtle hints that they think I shouldn't be returning to work."

"You see a lot on social media about how celebs seem to manage both their career and parenthood – I think it puts a warped view and unhelpful expectations on how you can balance both."

Depending on your team or organisation you may also be experiencing a culture of always-on & presenteeism, with both real and perceived judgements about how you are juggling your dual role.

"I'm paranoid that when I get up and walk out at five o'clock, everyone's judging me; this presenteeism culture, it's so pervasive in this part of the organisation, it feels very old school."

Finally, depending on the organisation, returning mothers can also experience male-dominated environments, which may have less experience of the challenges of returning from parental leave, particularly as fathers taking paternity leave is still very much a minority. Clients I've worked with in industries that have a significantly higher percentage of males to females tend to be more likely to experience challenges or a lack of understanding around juggling both work and parenting responsibilities.

The strategies to help manage this final set of challenges around the culture and norms of the organisation, whether as a mother or father, are covered in the next chapter: *Chapter 4: The initial return.*

The cultural challenge for fathers

Much has been explored about the concept of the *fatherhood bonus* and *motherhood penalty*, with research[17] indicating that upon becoming parents, fathers are seen in a more favourable light with increased employability and promotion prospects, whilst mothers are seen as less reliable, employable or competent. However, as fathers move into greater involvement with their children, such as taking shared parental leave (SPL) or working part-time, these benefits of the fatherhood bonus fade and dads can face stigmatisation and discrimination.[18]

Recent UK research[19] suggests that although there are thankfully more egalitarian views of parenting, having both parents working and being involved at home is now considered more the norm, there are still strong cultural drivers that perpetuate the notion of males as the main breadwinner, leading to challenges when changes to working patterns or taking SPL is requested by fathers. This UK research, conducted through interviews with managers and working parents, identifies three main types of cultural challenge, or "fatherhood forfeits", dads can face when they shift away from the gendered norm of breadwinner and take on more child-caring duties.

The first challenge is experiencing mockery or teasing from peers and managers. Although this may be perceived by those making the comments as "friendly banter", in reality there can be an element of menace attached to these comments. The second challenge is being viewed suspiciously or abnormal by others, with cynicism from other staff about working part-time or taking leave. The final cultural challenge is being perceived as idle or less committed, with an assumption that the fathers who work part-time were sitting around doing nothing whilst they weren't at work and didn't have the same commitment to their job as those working full-time or not taking leave. The research showed that although comments and views aren't generally maliciously intended, they do have a negative impact on working fathers who take SPL or work part-time.

To help counteract these challenges, as a father it's helpful to think through how you want to respond to any comments you may receive and reflect on the benefits for you and your family of taking SPL or working part-time. Whilst for managers the recommendations are to educate staff on the impacts of "friendly banter", champion examples of role modelling by working fathers and provide strategies to equip fathers to deal with comments.

Back in Chapter 1 we talked about the five types of support for those returning from parental leave: National, Organisation, Leader, Team and Self-support. The rest of this chapter focuses on what support is available to tackle the various challenges mentioned above, firstly considering Self-support, how as a returner you can help yourself, before looking at Leader or manager support, acknowledging the shared responsibility.

It is worth recognising for both returning parents and their managers, there are other types of support you can tap into. National support will depend on the country you are in and could include maternity and paternity pay and Keeping in Touch days; these types of support are explored later in this chapter. Additionally, there are various types of Organisation support and Team support which are detailed in *Chapter 5: Support from HR and the broader organisation.*

The returner's perspective

To help manage the variety of challenges you may face as a returning parent, there are a number of strategies you can adopt. The following section as part of Chapter 3, considers strategies *before* the return to work, which includes getting practicalities sorted, handling common emotions, keeping in contact and choosing how to return. The next chapter, *Chapter 4: The initial return*, details strategies to consider *once you're back* in the workplace, covering: creating priorities and boundaries, cognitive coping, and reaching out. For those that like seeing things visually, the following diagram illustrates how the strategies map onto the various challenges.

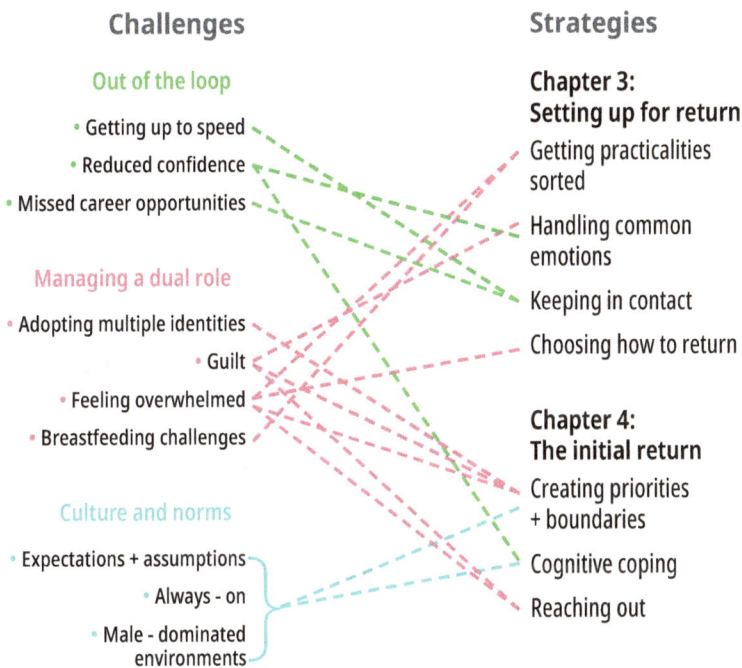

Challenges   Strategies

Out of the loop

* Getting up to speed
* Reduced confidence
* Missed career opportunities

Managing a dual role

* Adopting multiple identities
* Guilt
* Feeling overwhelmed
* Breastfeeding challenges

Culture and norms

* Expectations + assumptions
* Always - on
* Male - dominated environments

Chapter 3:
Setting up for return

Getting practicalities sorted

Handling common emotions

Keeping in contact

Choosing how to return

Chapter 4:
The initial return

Creating priorities + boundaries

Cognitive coping

Reaching out

Figure 6: Mapping challenges and strategies.

Getting practicalities sorted

To help manage the challenge of feeling overwhelmed, many returning parents talk about the benefits of getting organised before going back to the workplace. There are four main types of practicalities that can be helpful for you to consider: child-related, domestic, self-care and work-related.

Child-related practicalities

Finding suitable childcare is one of the most frequently cited problems for working parents so it is worth investigating early, especially as the most popular options tend to have long waiting lists and may need booking as soon as you or your partner get pregnant. When running pregnancy and parenting workshops I often find that soon-to-be parents are surprised when others in the group have already thought about their childcare as they were assuming that would be one of the things they'd consider when off on parental leave. It can be a shock to find out from others that the nursery close to work that they'd banked on getting into has a waiting list of over a year.

When thinking through your options, setting up childcare that feels right for you and your family can help alleviate the guilt on returning to work, rather than making assumptions about what's important.

> "I really wanted to go for the nursery that was just round the corner but there was another one that was open 30 minutes earlier so I went for that instead so I could get into work earlier. In retrospect, half an hour really wouldn't have made a difference, and I've regretted my choice."

Childcare can be divided roughly into care provided inside your own home with a nanny or au pair, or childcare that is outside of your home with childminders & nurseries. As a parent you may also end up drawing on your relatives for part or all of your childcare. If you are asking your extended family for help with childcare it's worth having early conversations about what level of support they are happy to provide so that they feel they are a help but don't feel over-burdened. There are pros and cons for each of the different types of childcare and, if you're not relying on family members, they are subject to different levels of supervision and regulation by the authorities.

If you are planning on working from home for some or all of the time, it's also worth considering the impact of having childcare based in your own home, as for many the emotional pull of hearing your baby makes it hard to focus on work.

> "I could hear my mum downstairs playing with Noah and I just wanted to go down and join them, I found it so hard and in the end, we decided it was better if my mum looked after him in her own house."

If you are working from home, it's also worth recognising that for the vast majority of working parents you will still need childcare as it's not possible to work at home and look after a baby.

"I'd assumed that I'd be able to work from home a couple of days and have my baby here with me and save on the costs of childcare, but you were so right, there's no way I could contemplate doing both. I tried and found that attempting calls with the noise of my baby in the background was really distracting and it felt like I wasn't paying proper attention to either work or my child."

The key with any childcare arrangement is choosing an option where you feel happy that your child will be safe and loved, which can then help to ease any potential guilt. There are lots of guidelines online to help you with choosing your childcare such as: https://www.familyandchildcaretrust.org/five-steps-choosing-childcare in the UK and https://childcare.gov/consumer-education/choosing-quality-childcare in the U.S.

When thinking about childcare it's also worth considering any assumptions you may have about what's the best childcare solution for your family and be open-minded to alternatives.

"I always assumed that nursery would be best for my daughter as I really didn't want to have someone in my house, however, I saw other mums doing a nanny-share and actually think that would have been a better option."

When planning childcare, it's helpful to think through how you will co-ordinate with your partner if you have one. For example, who is going to take responsibility at the beginning and end of the day for handover with your childcare provider?

Also think through your back-up childcare options. Childminders and nurseries won't take children if they're poorly, and there's a possibility that your childcarer could be ill or isolating with a virus, so it's helpful to think through who you could draw on in an emergency, as well as checking on your company policy around time off if you need to take care of a sick child. Again, if you have a partner, what are the agreements you have between you around who's going to be called upon first if, or rather when, your child is sick.

"I find it frustrating that although the nursery has numbers for both me and my husband, it always seems to be the mum that they call first when our child is ill and needs picking up early."

As I was recently reminded by one of my coaching colleagues, it's also worth not beating yourself up if you do end up having to take the odd day off when your child is sick.

"I remember back when I was returning to work, my son was ill on my first day back and I wasn't able to go into work. Although I was lucky because I had a very understanding manager, I really felt like any professionalism I had came crashing down."

Domestic practicalities

Although sorting domestic things may not be that exciting, getting organised and thinking about how to make your life easier at home can also help with the challenge of feeling overwhelmed when you return to work.

"I really tried to make things easier at home, so we got a cleaner and we tried to make a meal plan, so we'd have less dithering around in the evenings after work, the sort of stuff to just make the mechanics of it all a bit easier."

Different options to consider, to help you feel a bit more organised, include:

- using online grocery shopping, with shopping lists for common meals
- batch cooking and popping in the freezer
- thinking through how to share the domestic workload with your partner if you have one
- sorting household tasks, such as paying bills, car MOTs, fixing that leaking tap etc. – thinking through what you can tick off your to-do list before you start back
- getting a cleaner, if financially feasible
- going for good enough – working out which domestic chores you do to an unnecessarily high standard and scaling back

What's going for good enough?

For most of your life you've probably been encouraged to achieve your best, whether that was your teachers at school encouraging you to aim for "personal best" or a presentation you're doing for a client where you want it to be of the highest quality. It may be that you've always had some perfectionist tendencies, which although can sometimes be helpful, when you're trying to juggle the combined responsibilities of home, work and your children, it's normally better to adopt a more pragmatic approach.

Research[20] and common sense indicates that if you try to do everything to a very high standard it can cause unnecessary stress and actually be counterproductive. The trick is to determine which areas of life you are able to go for "good enough" and avoid perfectionist tendencies.

The 80:20 rule, or Pareto principle, can be helpful when considering where to cut back. The theory is that for certain situations, 20% of your effort produces 80% of the results, whilst the remaining 80% of effort only produces an extra 20% of the results. For example, if I have my mother-in-law coming over and I want to give the impression that my house isn't a complete tip, I'm going to focus on cleaning the living room, kitchen and downstairs toilet and not worry about the mess in all the other rooms that is not likely to be seen.

In practical terms it means thinking through where you are doing things to an unnecessarily high standard and what is "good enough" instead. Do you need to be doing that level of home-cooked food, ironing, cleaning, washable nappies etc, or could you be kinder to yourself and reduce some of your standards.

> *"One of the best pieces of advice I had when returning a second time was to let my older kid live on cheese sandwiches when they came back from nursery. It really helped not to put additional pressure on myself, and I knew they were getting a cooked meal at their nursery."*

When I'm working with coaching clients before they go back to work, we normally discuss which areas of their domestic life if any, they want to hang onto high standards, for example, having freshly cooked food and which they can drop, e.g. ironing anything other than work clothes.

Self-care

Although it may sound frivolous, it's worth thinking about other activities to squeeze in before return. This could include personal care such as haircut, dentist or other appointments, time to catch up with friends, relatives or to exercise, or anything else that helps you take care of yourself and set you up for the best return. Although these can still be fitted in once you've returned, the initial few months of transition will feel more hectic and therefore harder to find time for all those extra things in your life.

Some parents have also treated themselves to new clothes or accessories to help mentally make that transition from stay-at-home parent to working parent.

> *"It may sound trivial, but I treated myself to a new posh bag, so that I was very clearly making that step from being a mum lugging around a change-bag stuffed with nappies, to adopting my work persona again."*

It's also worth considering your own settling-in plan. There are normally settling-in plans for your infant at their childcare setting, but many returning parents I talk to haven't considered it for themselves. For example, finding time to do a trial run of the morning routine, getting both yourself and your child ready and then handing over your child to their daily childcare will help you figure out how things are going to work and make the transition back easier. Keeping in contact, which is covered later in this chapter, is also an important part of settling back into work.

Work-related practicalities

The final area of practicalities is thinking through work logistics. The challenge that returning parents often underestimate is getting back up to speed and handling the practicalities of returning to the workplace. In some cases, returners may have managers who have thought this through, but it's wise to assume that the onus is on you. If you can sort out as much as possible before your return, then it will help avoid any extra hiccups when you're back.

> *"I made sure that before I came back my systems were all set up in a way that I could just pick up from where I left off."*

In practice, things that you may have to sort out could include your work pass, having full access back onto computer systems, signing back up to email lists, your phone connection and if you're a breastfeeding mum, how you're going to express back at work.

Handling common emotions

The previous chapter talked about managing the transition from being a working professional to stay-at-home parent when you go off on parental leave. Even with short periods of leave there is then an adjustment back into the workplace, reorientating yourselves towards work and considering how you successfully combine parenthood with your work and career. Although there can be a sense of excitement and anticipation about returning to work, looking forward to having more adult conversations and using other parts of your brain again, it can also throw up less helpful emotions.

> *"I'm really looking forward to going back and using parts of my brain that I haven't challenged in the last six months, however, I'm feeling a bit scared about whether I'm still going to be as good as I was before."*

The return to work can throw up many concerns for working parents. From my own research and talking to a wide cross-section of parents over the years, the most common emotions experienced during the transition of returning to work are lack of confidence, feeling overwhelmed and a sense of guilt.

> *"I'm not sure how I'm going to cope when I go back as there are days when I'm struggling now, and I'm not also having to manage my workload."*

There are three main strategies that returning parents have found useful to help with handling these common emotions: firstly, a reality check on concerns, secondly managing expectations and finally emotionally preparing to leave.

Reality check on concerns

Similar to the exercise suggested in the previous chapter, as you start to think about returning to work, it can be helpful to reflect on what your concerns are. Once you've identified any potential concerns, doing a reality check on how true these actually are or spotting whether you've fallen into the trap of catastrophising. Then thinking about how you can reframe your concern and what actions to put in place. For example, I've heard many parents talk about concerns with managing their morning schedule, and although mornings can be tricky, these concerns can sometimes be overblown after hearing horror stories from other parents. A helpful action could be to do a trial run, potentially combining with a connecting in day back in the workplace.

Similarly, for some of your concerns or unhelpful emotions it's useful to think about how you can reframe them. For example, you may be feeling guilty because you believe that you are lowering your standards at home and not doing things how you would like to be doing them. Instead, you could reframe. Recognising that your time is limited, rather than thinking you are not meeting standards, you are instead going for "good enough" to free up time elsewhere – I'm choosing to have time to play with my child rather than ironing pants. Using a table, such as the example below, can be a useful tool to help think through the steps.

Table 2: Reality check.

Concern	Reality check or reframe	Action
How am I going to be able to manage in the mornings?	I recognise that it's going to be tricky, but I know that I can get organised.	I'm going to do a trial run, dropping off at nursery and then going into work.
I feel guilty that I'm lowering my standards by going for "good enough".	There are only so many hours in the day, and by cutting out the ironing I know have more time to play with my daughter.	Aim to block out 1 on 1 playtime every day with my child.
I'm worried I'm not going to be as good at work as I was before.	Although it may take me a while to get up to speed, the skills I had before haven't disappeared, I am still someone that's very organised.	I'm going to write myself a list of the skills I know I had at work and keep reminding myself of them.
Other concerns:		

Managing expectations

A second strategy for handling common emotions is to do a sense check on the expectations you have of yourself on returning to work and whether they are fair and realistic. These are often expressed as the "shoulds" and "shouldn'ts" you are giving yourself:

> *"I should be on top of everything and shouldn't be dropping the ball."*

> *"I should be there for all of my baby's milestones and shouldn't miss them because I'm going back to work."*

> *"I should be able to quickly slot back into work and perform at the same level."*

Acknowledging where you have high or unrealistic expectations of yourself can help alleviate feelings of guilt. By recognising what these expectations are, and doing a sense check on whether they're fair, can help you reframe and think about where you should be going for good enough or being kinder to yourself. A good sense check is to see whether you would have the same expectations for someone else – are you being harder on yourself, expecting super-mum or super-dad, compared to how you think other working parents manage the transition back?

It can sometimes be tricky to spot where you are putting unfair or unrealistic expectations on yourself. If that's the case it's helpful to get feedback from family or friends, who may more easily spot where you are developing unhelpful self-expectations.

This isn't saying don't set any expectations or standards for yourself upon your return to work, or that you should expect to be given an easy ride on your return; but more, do a sense check, as many returning parents set themselves unhelpfully high expectations, which actually causes more stress and means the transition back takes longer.

Emotionally preparing to leave

For some going back to work can feel a bit of a relief after the intensity of staying at home and baby talk, whilst for others it can feel a real wrench leaving their child with someone else whilst they work.

> "When I dropped my little one off for her trial at nursery I just sat in the park and cried, I found it really hard to leave her and just felt like a rubbish mum."

Thinking about how to ease that separation can help if you are experiencing anxiety about leaving your child when you return. What are the strategies you can adopt to emotionally prepare yourself? For example, this could be leaving your child as part of the settling in at their childcare, getting a babysitter and planning nights out with your partner or friends, or arranging to leave your baby with others for a while.

> "I was feeling very anxious about leaving her, so for about a month before I was due back, I did try and leave the baby with others for an hour or two to start the process [of leaving them], which did help."

These three strategies – a reality check on concerns, managing expectations and emotionally preparing to leave – are all strategies for managing your emotions as you prepare to return. In the next chapter there is a section on cognitive coping mechanisms, which are additional strategies once you have returned to work.

Keeping in contact

The third set of strategies to think through in preparation for returning to work, is how you keep in contact. Keeping in touch with colleagues whilst off on parental leave has a number of benefits, including helping reduce the time you take to transition back in, allowing you to get up to speed with changes and also helping you connect back in with people.

"I was anxious about coming back in, whether people would still want me, and were the people who were stepping in for me better than me? Coming in definitely took that away a little bit, helping me feel that I was still valued, and also being kept in the loop."

Whether that's coming in for team days, training, IT updates, communications events or just connecting in with people, keeping in touch can help it feel less of a transition when returning to the workplace.

It is worth thinking about when during your parental leave you want to start making those connections back into the workplace, to avoid feeling that you need to keep in regular contact all the way through, but at the other extreme not leaving it until just before you return. In practice most returning parents find that it's useful to start the process of connecting in around three quarters of the way through their parental leave, so if you are taking a year's leave, two to three months before returning. Or for example if you are taking 10 weeks, the average time in the U.S., then starting to make that contact two to three weeks before returning.

"I kept in touch informally with lots of people across the wider team, so they knew when I was returning. That meant I had a couple of people looking out for me on my first few days back."

If your job relies on building external client relationships, there may also be communications you want to start up with them to help smooth the transition. It's also worth thinking about how you want to keep in contact with your manager and others in the workplace to discuss potential roles and career path on returning, this can help with the challenges of feeling that you have missed out on career opportunities because of not being in contact. There is more in the next section on thinking about your role and how you want to return.

Using KIT or SPLIT days

Since 2007, those on maternity or adoption leave in the UK have been entitled to take up to 10 mutually agreed Keeping in Touch (KIT) days back at work or in training, without impacting their entitlement to statutory maternity leave and pay, or adoption leave. Similarly, the introduction of Shared Parental Leave, since 2015, also allows up to 20 Shared Parental Leave in Touch (SPLIT) days.

Although some returners have just used these days as a financial boost whilst off on leave, coming back in and doing their job, parents that have used them more strategically have found they can help overcome some of the challenges of returning to work.

> *"The KIT days helped me the most in terms of support for coming back; they helped reconnect me back to the office and connect in with stakeholders. Using my KIT days to come in 1 day a month also helped me to be visible, which felt really important if I was going to be considered for promotion."*

For more details on your entitlement and using KIT and SPLIT days, Maternity Action has a great Q&A section on their website: https://maternityaction.org.uk/advice/keeping-in-touch-days/. Additionally in Chapter 5 there are strategies for how HR and the organisation can best support the use of KIT and SPLIT days.

If you live outside of the UK and don't have this as part of your legislation or as a company initiative, it is still worth thinking about how you can make that connection back into the workplace to help ease your transition.

Choosing how to return

The final set of strategies to help you set up for the best return is thinking through *how* you want to return. This section firstly explores making decisions around your working hours and role on return and then secondly, considers how you may want to phase your return to work.

Deciding working hours and role

The decision around your working hours is a very personal one and ideally is based on what feels right for you and your family, rather than based on societal pressures or norms. I have seen parents feel happy with their choice to go back part-time and equally those that who are happy to go back full-time. But likewise, those same choices have felt wrong for other parents. Clearly there are also some parents that feel the right decision for them is to take a career break and not go back at this stage.

Legally in many countries you have to be offered the same or an equivalent role when you return. If you want more details on your rights, good websites include ACAS in the UK: https://www.acas.org.uk/your-maternity-leave-pay-and-other-rights/returning-to-work-after-having-a-baby and Family Education website in

U.S.: https://www.familyeducation.com/pregnancy/maternity-leave/maternity-leave-laws-what-are-your-rights

You may be looking to return with the same working hours and role, however, many returning parents want to consider the options for different types of roles and/or working hours. For most working parents it comes down to balancing three areas: fulfilment, finances and flexibility. Ideally you can achieve all of these, but in practice there may have to be trade-offs and so understanding what's important to you will help you achieve the balance of these three that feels right for you.

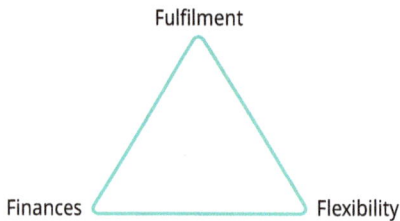

Fulfilment

Finances   Flexibility

Figure 7: Achieving the balance – the 3 Fs.

Firstly, how important is it to have a sense of fulfilment or satisfaction from your job at this stage in your career. For some they feel that if they are going to be spending time away from their child, then it needs to be doing something that feels fulfilling whilst for others having more flexibility is important. To illustrate this the quotes below are from two parents who both worked within the same financial organisation.

> Parent 1: *"I know that my career is really important to me, and if I'm going to be at work and away from her [my daughter] then I need to be doing something that feels worthwhile and meaningful. I can't do this role part-time and recognise that I need to sacrifice some of the flexibility that I would get from working reduced hours to get that sense of buzz from my work."*

> Parent 2: *"So when I was considering what roles I wanted to go for when I returned to work, I thought long and hard about what was important to me. So, the position I've ended up in isn't the kind of role I would want longer term, but it works brilliantly for now as it allows me to work normal hours rather than the stupid hours I was doing before."*

Ideally you can agree with your manager a role that feels both fulfilling and meaningful whilst working the hours that give you the flexibility you want, but you may find, at least in the short-term, that there is some trade-off you need to make to achieve the balance of flexibility and fulfilment that feels right for you.

The other consideration is how important finances are to you. You may choose and be financially stable enough to reduce your hours, whereas for others there will be a need, or a choice, to continue to work full-time, and reduce their flexibility as they feel that's the only way to keep the type of fulfilling role and income level they want.

> *"I didn't even consider the possibility of working part-time; I don't think you can do a job like mine [working in investment banking] and have that kind of flexibility. I did fleetingly consider taking a massive pay cut and changing roles, but that's not for me."*

> *"I would love to be able to work less hours, but we're dependent on my income to make the mortgage payments and I just don't see a way I could feasibly work less."*

When discussing the options for how you want to return with your manager and/ or HR, it's worth thinking through how you can meet both your needs and those of the organisation, seeing flexibility as a two-way street. For making a flexible working request in the UK there are a couple of helpful resources from both ACAS: https://www.acas.org.uk/making-a-flexible-working-request and also CIPD: https://www.cipd.co.uk/knowledge/fundamentals/relations/flexible-working/re questing-flexible-working-guide

To help you with your decisions around how to return, there are three main tactics to consider:

– Checking your assumptions
– Understanding expectations
– Recognise it's not a permanent choice

Checking what assumptions you may be making can be a helpful first tactic, whether that's assumptions on what you think is feasible in your workplace, assumptions around what your partner may be thinking or assumptions that you've made for yourself because you think you need to follow a route that others have taken. These are some of the assumptions I've heard during my coaching sessions:

> *"I don't think that type of flexible working is possible where I work as no-one has done it before."*

"Ah, I hadn't thought to question how I believed my husband would pull his weight at home, I was assuming we'd equally split things, particularly when I go back to work."

"There's a norm in this organisation that you don't take a full year of maternity leave, no-one else has, and so I was assuming I was going to go back after nine months, which seems to be the most that others have taken off."

Our brains can often make assumptions as a shortcut, so it can be worth challenging what those are and seeing whether it's more helpful to test those assumptions out and view things in a different light. For example, if you're making assumptions about what type of flexible work is possible, have a discussion with HR and your manager to see what alternatives there are.

Secondly, recognise where you might be bowing to expectations from others, rather than doing what feels right for you.

"I felt a lot of pressure from my mother-in-law not to go back to work as she didn't work when she had children, but I genuinely don't think I'd be as good a mother if I didn't have that outlet of work as well. Although I am a bit worried about whether that makes me a bad mother because my career is also important to me."

To help with any pressure you might be feeling to make certain choices, it's useful to avoid comparing yourself to others, and surround yourself with people who have made similar choices to you, whether that's working full-time, part-time or choosing not to go back. As parents we can feel guilty for choosing any of these options, but that's normally when we compare ourselves to others.

The final tactic is to recognise that whatever choice you make, it doesn't need to be a permanent one. This phase in your life, the early years of parenthood, is relatively short compared to your overall career span. For mothers that have decided to take a career break there are some great resources out there to help with returning after a longer break including "She's back" by Lisa Unwin and Deb Khan and the website Women Returners found at: https://womenreturners.com/. For dads, the UK Fatherhood Institute (http://www.fatherhoodinstitute.org/) provides some great resources.

Once you have settled back into work you may want to re-think the balance of these three areas: fulfilment, flexibility and finances. There are more details in *Chapter 6: Moving forwards*, to help you think about how you want to manage your career and the balance that's important for you.

But I feel I have to return

Some parents feel they have no choice about how they go back, with financial pressure meaning that although they would prefer to be spending more time at home with their little one, they feel they either have to return and/or do more hours than they would like.

> *"The current cost of living crisis means I really feel like I have no choice, I would much prefer to be taking longer maternity leave but just can't afford to."*

If this is your situation, the suggestion is to firstly check your financial assumptions on what is feasible and the options for reducing living costs that would allow you to reduce work hours or not work at all. Some of the options may feel drastic such as moving house and potentially location, or taking in lodgers, however, it can help to recognise that these are potential choices or options, and that you are choosing to stay at work even if it's only because the other options seem even worse.

There is long-established psychological research, self-determination theory,[21] which shows the importance of having autonomy and feeling we have a sense of control or choice. If we feel we lack this autonomy and choice, then this can lead to stress and lack of well-being. Therefore, recognising there are alternative choices, even if they seem very undesirable, can help bring back a sense of control and reduce stress levels.

Coaching clients of mine have felt less stressed when their mindset is "I'd prefer not to go back, but I'm choosing to work because financially the other options are less desirable" rather than thinking "I have no choice, I have to go back". Thinking through the upsides of your choice to go back to work can also help alleviate stress levels, reflecting on the benefits that work can bring to you and your family, and recognising the positives that your baby or infant can get from their childcare setting. Again, it is less stressful to be thinking "there are some real benefits for my child going to nursery, such as learning sociability skills" rather than having a mindset of "my child is only in nursery because I have to go back to work." I recognise this is often easier said than done but trying to change your mindset can really help.

Phasing return to work

Once you've agreed your working hours and role for when you return, it's worth considering whether and how you can phase your return back to the workplace. Phasing your return is a good way to help counteract the challenges of feeling overwhelmed and getting up to speed. Whether you choose to use holiday, or within the UK use KIT/SPLIT days, many parents find it helpful to phase in their return to work. In practice this means that rather than starting back and working all of the days you've agreed to do each week, instead, you build up over a period of time to the number of days you are finally going to do. The same principle applies whether you are choosing to go back full-time or part-time.

There are clearly a wide variety of ways to do this, whether that's a couple of weeks or months using holiday to do one or two days a week, or whether the number of days worked is slowly built up over time. A couple of examples are given below:

> *"I came back for two days, then three days then up to four days over a month or so and I found that really helpful to adjust back into work, rather than going straight back into four days."*

> *"I chose to come back full-time but I didn't want to go straight into full-time work as that felt like too much of a shock, so I used my holiday for the last three weeks of my maternity leave to come in for two days a week. That helped me to get back up to speed without the team or my boss starting to pile too much work onto me."*

If you experience guilt and sadness at leaving your baby, a phased return can also help with mentally preparing yourself for that transition back to work.

> *"A phased return was my way of controlling my emotions and preparing mentally for going back. So, it was kind of, I've just got to get through today, just through today, and then I've got a whole week before I have to go in again and then I'm with my daughter so we're going to do these fun things. The next week it was then two days working then time with my daughter. So, I think that slow build-up meant that it wasn't too much of a change psychologically and mentally."*

Some parents also use holiday or KIT days to return to work part-time without taking a drop in salary. This can then be used to see whether part-time or flexible working fits well with the role you're going back into.

"I did a four-day week for a couple of months, using holiday, as a bit of a test to see how I found that. I didn't want to agree to a four-day week as part of my contract from the start as I didn't want that 20% drop in my salary."

However, it is worth really thinking about what suits you best as some parents come back full-time and wish they'd phased a return.

"I came back full-time into a brand-new job, with a new team and that I think suited me at the time. I'm the kind of rip off the plaster quickly kind of person . . . Although maybe I should have phased in a little bit more and kind of gone under the radar a bit so that I could spend those early days catching up . . . You know if I could do it again, maybe I'd think about doing that, rather than big bang, full blast, into a new job."

Whilst other parents do phase a return and find that it knocks their confidence, finding it hard to make that switch between work and parental roles.

"When I came back I built it up, so I did two days for two weeks, three days for three weeks and then up to four days. I found it really difficult because I wasn't in the most confident of places, and I found it really hard to manage my team. I think I saw it as a bit of a sign of weakness that I wasn't there to lead them. I also found it hard to create a rhythm and a routine, because I was in for two days, and I was kind of ready to go in on the third day, but then it was like, no, take that hat off and put your mummy hat back on."

When choosing how to return, whether that's around your role and hours or how you will phase back to work, if you are part of a couple, it's important to have discussions with your partner, so there is joint decision-making around how as a family you can support both your baby and each other in your careers. The types of questions it can be helpful to ask are:

–   Are you both going to go back to work or is one of you going to stay at home for a period of time?
–   If you're both back at work what's the balance between you on working full or part-time?
–   If both working full-time, what's the balance on managing when your child is sick?

If you are UK based, it's also worth considering whether you want to use Shared Parental Leave if you haven't already; from the research I've done and from working with my coaching clients, it can provide great benefits to you as a family.

"I feel very lucky that my transition was made much easier by the fact that when I first went back on both occasions my kids were at home with my husband. I didn't have the stress about leaving them at childcare or worry about how they were settling in. He also did the night feeds, so I had sleep on my side when I went back to work; that was definitely a benefit."

"Of all the different sources of support I got during my transition back into work, my partner taking Shared Parental Leave was definitely the most useful. It was such a help and meant that a big part of the anxiety of returning was relieved. I also think it was a great time for the two of them to bond."

If you are in a leadership role and/or working within HR, there are more details on how to encourage the use of leave for fathers in *Chapter 5: Support from HR and the broader organisation*. Finally, if considering career management as a couple, a great resource I often recommend is "Couples that work" by Jennifer Petriglieri,[22] one of the professors from my business school, INSEAD. This book has lots of case studies, exercises and strategies on how to thrive as a dual career couple.

The manager's perspective

When discussing with both returning parents and their managers about what support is most effective and useful to help the transition back into the workplace, five areas consistently come up as important to consider before the return to work:

- Communications
- Setting up flexible working
- Career planning
- Sorting practical aspects
- Empathy and advice

The rest of this chapter looks at how as a manager you can support your returning parent in these five areas as they prepare to return to work, with a checklist at the end as a helpful summary.

Communications

Hopefully you have already agreed the type and level of communication with your returner during their period of leave. Typically, there are three broad types of communication that are helpful to consider:

- Significant updates or organisational changes that impact them.
- Team events, training or other important decision-making meetings they may want to attend.
- Conversations around plans for return including date, role and working pattern.

Although your returning parent probably won't want to be kept updated throughout their parental leave, to help with the sense of information overload and feeling overwhelmed when they first return, it's useful to keep them up to date, particularly during the last quarter of their parental leave.

> "It would have been good if my boss had spent a bit of time when I came in [for my KIT days] to keep me up to date with what's changed. Just 20 mins, half an hour, a quick run through would have been useful."

One-off events, such as team days, can also be a useful way of getting your returner up to speed and connected in with others. If you are inviting the returner in for one-off events, it's helpful to let them know the agenda or format of the day so that they can manage their childcare logistics.

> *"It was good to be able to come in for the annual sales planning day and they let me know which bits of the day would be most useful for me to attend; that was really helpful as it would have been tricky logistically to come for the whole day."*

As well as communications to keep the returner up to date and include them in events or meetings, the other important area to discuss are plans for return. As well as agreeing the date for return, it's important to discuss how they want to return. If you've not already read it, there are lots of details in the previous section, *Choosing how to return*, on the areas to discuss with your returning parent including helping them decide their working hours and role and also whether to phase their return to work.

Setting up flexible working

The returning parent you're managing may want to return with the same working pattern they had before they went on parental leave, but for many parents their dual responsibilities means that they want to consider how they can work flexibly so that they prioritise both their work and family.

Depending on the country you're based in, there may be regulations around the right to ask for flexible working which you should be aware of e.g. as most managers in the UK will know, there is now the right to ask for flexible working from the start of your employment.[23] There are also many easily accessible guides to help through the practical and legal aspects (e.g. in UK, the ACAS guide: https://www.acas.org.uk/acas-code-of-practice-on-flexible-working-requests/html).

Some organisations have a culture and set-up that means it's easier to accommodate flexible working requests, whereas managers in other organisations have faced a variety of different challenges:

> *"My returner doesn't seem to understand that flexible working is a two-way street."*

> *"I'm getting push back from others in the team that I'm making allowances for newly returned parents."*

> *"I'm really not sure how I'm going to manage the priorities of the business with part-time working."*

When considering flexible working requests there is clearly a balance between managing the needs of the business and the needs of the individual. There are some practical things you can do as a manager when setting up flexible working for parental returners, or indeed for anyone in your team who's considering a flexible work pattern. Below are the areas to consider *before* return, whilst the next chapter looks at guidelines to support flexible working *after* the returning parent is back in work.

Before return:

- Develop clear expectations from both sides including *key-to-have* compared to *nice-to-have.*
- Don't be restricted by what's gone before – it's not one size fits all.
- Adjust the role to the fit the flexible pattern rather than trying to squeeze a full-time role into part-time hours.
- Understand the benefits of flexible working e.g. motivation, well-being, retention. There is a great evidence-based paper from the UK-based CIPD, detailing the various benefits: https://www.cipd.co.uk/knowledge/fundamentals/rela tions/flexible-working/cross-sector-insights-guide

When there is support from the manager for flexible working, it can have a significant impact on the individual.

> *"I worked for a guy who's the father of two very young children with a wife who worked four days. That was really good for me because his wife had a really high-level job, so he had the appreciation that four days is normal for a working mum. That was what I heard from him and what I felt from him, which was really reassuring. That was a pocket of real goodness, despite the organisation as a whole not feeling supportive."*

The final area to consider around flexible working is helping the returner to think about how / if they want to phase back into the workplace as it may be something they haven't considered.

> *"My maternity returner seemed surprised when I asked her how she wanted to come back, whether that was full-steam or glide back in. She thought she didn't have the option, that she had to come back operating at the same rate as before from day one."*

Details of the different ways returners can phase back in is covered earlier in the chapter.

Career planning

Connected to any flexible working requests is having discussions with your re-turning parent around the role that they are coming back into. It may be that they're returning to exactly the same role or that there are changes based on the working patterns they're requesting.

> *"I made sure that when she [a maternity returner] came in for discussions dur-ing her mat leave that we had some time to think about her career options. I didn't want to put any pressure on her, but I wanted to understand her think-ing and how that fitted with the business."*

There may also be organisation changes that have happened whilst they're away and therefore as well as helping to keep them up to date with any changes, there may be new roles that you need to talk through with them or potentially inter-view them for. It's helpful to coordinate with your returner so the logistics of any discussions can run smoothly, for example if they're being interviewed giving them enough notice to organise childcare.

> *"There was a big org restructure that happened whilst she [my direct report] was off on maternity leave – we ended up doing the interviews for her new role over Teams whilst she had her baby with her, which made it trickier."*

It can be useful to keep an open mind about potential roles, as for some returners they may not have clear ideas themselves until they get back into work.

> *"I felt like I got it really wrong, my returner had said that she wanted to have some new challenging projects when she got back and so that's what we ar-ranged, but in reality she actually found it a bit overwhelming at first, I really think I should have checked in more and delayed that work a bit."*

For both career planning support and flexible working support, as a manager it's helpful to ask yourself what assumptions you may be making, whether that's the type of role they want to go for, the level of challenge they're looking for or how they want to return.

Sorting practical aspects

It's been suggested in the returner's perspective that they think through the logis-tics and practical aspects of their return, however, if you or a support person within your team have capacity, it can be a quick win to organise getting those things sorted so that there is a smoother transition back.

> *"My manager organised for all the practical things to be sorted like access to a locker, a laptop and pass and stuff like that, which I wouldn't have thought of and just made life much easier when I came back."*

It can be helpful to think of your returner as a new employee, since although they may have already been in the business / your department, having been out for a while there are likely to have been changes and they may not be aware of new systems and processes. Any changes that have happened whilst they have been out of the business will have happened more gradually for those that are still within work, but coming back after a period of being away means it hits the returner all in one go.

Empathy and advice

The level of empathy and advice you provide before your returner returns can be a tricky balance, since, as described in the previous chapter, offering emotional support, empathy or advice can be misinterpreted, with leavers or returners perceiving the comments as them being seen as not capable. However, the majority of people I've spoken to or worked with have really appreciated this type of support from their manager, as seen in the examples below.

> *"My manager was fantastic and the best thing he said to me was, 'You're going to come back next week, and you don't know how you're going to feel. You might feel delighted to be in the office and you know, be with grownups and having coffee and you shouldn't feel guilty if that's how you feel. Or you might come back to your desk and be in tears because you just want to be at home, and that's okay too. And if you feel like that, just go home, because it's a transition' and you know, that was the best thing for someone to say, because it gave me the freedom to not worry about how I was being perceived."*

> *"When I was due to come back after my maternity leave, I wasn't sure whether to go down the childminder, nanny, or nursery route and she'd [my manager] pretty much tried all of them, so it was good to have advice from her."*

A final area of potential advice is being aware of, and passing on details of, any relevant organisation initiatives that may be useful, such as buddy networks, parental returners training or support groups.

Asking the returning parent what type of support they want from you is the most direct way of understanding how to get the balance right, as it can be hard to put yourself in their shoes. However, they may not always have a clear understanding themselves, or feel uncomfortable explaining to you, so taking a bit of time to consider how your comments or input are received can also help you judge the level of emotional and practical support needed.

In summary when thinking about your role as a manager, the following thoughts from a UK Chief Executive I was recently chatting with can be helpful to bear in mind:

> *"Although it's potentially extra work accommodating parental returners, as a manger it's important to think about how it's much easier to retain talent than it is to recruit. I will bend over backwards for returning parents if I value their talent."*

Returning with additional challenges

When parents start to think through their return to the workplace they can experience a range of emotions from excitement, loss, shock, fear, guilt, worry, scepticism, uncertainty, acceptance and optimism. Coping with this normal range of emotions is picked up as part of *Handling common emotions* earlier in this chapter, however, sadly there can be situations which place an extra emotional burden on parents.

This section highlights experiences and resources to help cope with postnatal depression, babies with chronic illnesses and still births, with a strong recommendation to seek professional help if this is an area that is impacting you as a returning parent. Within the UK, therapists can be found via the NHS,[24] the British Association of Counsellors and Psychotherapists[25] (BACP) or the UK Council for Psychotherapy[26] (UKCP). There are a range of support groups, and personal recommendations from those who have gone through similar experiences is a good way of helping to find the right support for yourself.

Postnatal depression

Postnatal depression (or postpartum depression as it's known in the U.S.), is thought to affect more than 1 in 10 new mothers and although it's much less known about, can also affect almost the same percentage of fathers.[27] A great resource to understand more about this illness is the Royal College of Psychiatrists information page on postnatal depression, which can also be ordered as hard copy leaflet: https://www.rcpsych.ac.uk/mental-health/problems-disorders/postnatal-depression.

Their guidance highlights the important first step of recognising that you have a depressive illness and not dismiss it as the "baby blues" – feeling sad, tearful or anxious in the first week or two after giving birth. If symptoms persist longer than this then it may be an indication of postnatal depression and therefore important to speak to a healthcare professional.

Additional sources of information can be found both on the UK NHS website[28] and on the U.S. government,[29] and private clinic[30] websites.

Coping with chronic illness

When an infant goes into a childcare setting when their parents return to work, there is often a spike in the frequency of illnesses that they pick up, with parents often talking about the challenges they find with coping when their little one is poorly and managing the juggling between their professional and home life. Strategies covered in both this and the next chapter such as *Getting practicalities sorted* and *Creating priorities and boundaries* are designed to help with this more typical level of challenge such as feeling overwhelmed and a sense of guilt.

In the sad cases where an infant has a more serious illness or disability this clearly puts an additional emotional and practical burden on the parents, and although in many cases one or both of the parents may choose to delay the return to work, that may not be an option that works for your family. Suggested coping mechanisms include developing support networks, making time to care for yourself both mentally and physically, and recognising that feelings of guilt, anger and sadness are normal.

When someone very close to you is ill, it is common to develop feelings of being out of control, which can lead you to want to take to the internet and start searching to find out as much information as you can. If you haven't yet found online resources, good starting points are both the UK NHS[31] and the U.S. American Psychological Association[32] (APA).

Although taking practical action such as searching the internet, has been shown to reduce stress levels, there is a note of caution on how much research you do. Subjecting yourself to information overload or a sense of needing to do endless online searches can lead to additional stress.

Returning after the loss of a baby

Very sadly some babies are lost whilst the mother is pregnant, whilst giving birth or shortly afterwards. The latest research[33] shows that in the UK, one in four pregnancies ends in loss during pregnancy or birth, and although the majority of these are miscarriages (occurring before 24 weeks), of the 2000 babies born each day, seven are stillborn.

The UK charity Tommy's[34] provides a wealth of information and resources, whilst the U.S. organisation MEND[35] provides a detailed list of support organisations both national and state specific.

Supporting as a manager

This section has been written to provide resources and a sense of shared experience for the returning parent. If you are reading this as the manager of a returner, this will hopefully also act as a resource for you to guide and connect in with your parent. The ways that you can support your working parent that have already been outlined, namely communications, setting up flexible working, career planning, sorting practical aspects and providing empathy and advice will all still be applicable and of great use when supporting through any additional challenges.

Supporting after child loss

Supporting a parent after they have lost a child can feel a really tricky experience for managers, wanting to be supportive, but potentially not knowing the best way to help. The following case study from Sarah who worked as a Director within academia can hopefully help shed some light.

"We lost our baby after five months, whilst I was off on maternity leave, which was clearly a horrific thing to go through, but was definitely helped by how supportive and empathetic my manager was. The first thing my boss did was took me off maternity pay and put me onto sick pay which was amazing, and practically a great help. He was also really good at keeping in touch with me, asking me 'What do you need right now, and what's the most useful thing I can do?' I also felt I was given the time and space that I needed, with my manager telling me 'We don't mind what you do, just do whatever feels right for you, and talk to us when you feel ready.'

When it was time to have a conversation about what going back might look and feel like, they were incredibly flexible – there was a real sense of what are the possibilities we can create for this person whose world has been shattered, rather than what are the rules and what is the policy. It was such a weird time, and sometimes the conversations we had felt a bit like an out of body experience, it was only later that I fully realised how lucky I was to have such an amazing employer. It was being given that time, space, level of consideration and lack of pressure that really helped, and from a practical point of view effectively honouring my maternity leave for a year through putting me on sick pay."

Checklist

Below is a summary of the things to consider either as a returning parent or as their manager:

Returner's checklist	√
Have I sorted childcare?	
What options have I considered to make domestic life easier?	
What am I putting in place for self-care?	
Have I sorted work practicalities?	
What concerns do I need to reality check and potentially action?	
How can I ease any separation anxiety?	
What do I need to do to keep in touch?	
What balance of flexibility, finances and fulfilment am I looking for?	
Have I decided on my work hours and discussed with my manager / HR?	
What assumptions am I making about how I'll return?	
What type of phasing back to work is right for me?	

Manager's checklist	√
What comms do I need to be keeping my returner up to date with?	
How am I connecting in with my returner during any KIT or SPLIT days?	
What do I need to consider or manage in connection with flexible working?	
What assumptions am I making about my returner's career plans and aspirations?	
Have I had conversations about when and how they want to return and their career?	
What practical aspects e.g. pass, laptop etc needs to be in place?	
Am I providing the right level of empathy and advice?	
Are there any organisation initiatives that it's useful to inform my returner about?	

Chapter 4: The initial return

As a returning parent, you have hopefully already been able to leave work in the most effective way and have thought through how to come back in the strongest possible position. However, even if you have only picked up this book at the point of returning to work, there are still lots of practical strategies that help ease the transition back. As a manager there are also lots of areas to consider. This chapter covers:

–   Revisiting the challenges – reminder of the typical challenges faced on returning to work.
–   Returner's perspective – strategies once you've returned to the workplace: creating priorities and boundaries, cognitive coping, reaching out.
–   Manager's perspective – strategies for managers: communications, supporting flexible working, empathy and advice, role modelling.
–   Checklist – summary actions for returning parents and their managers.

Revisiting the challenges

Although it may feel slightly doom and gloom revisiting the challenges typically faced when returning to work, taking some time to reflect can help clarify some of the experiences you're having as a returning parent and also realise you're not alone. For managers, it can also be helpful to recap so that you can look out for signs of which challenges your returner is experiencing.

On the following page is a reminder of the potential challenges when coming back into the workplace after parental leave. Many of these challenges, can start to be tackled *before* returning, with a recap below of what was discussed in *Chapter 3: Setting up for return.*

–   Getting practicalities sorted and choosing how to return helps with *feeling overwhelmed.*
–   Handling common emotions helps with *reduced confidence* and *guilt.*
–   Keeping in contact helps with *getting up to speed* and *missed career opportunities.*

https://doi.org/10.1515/9783111618456-004

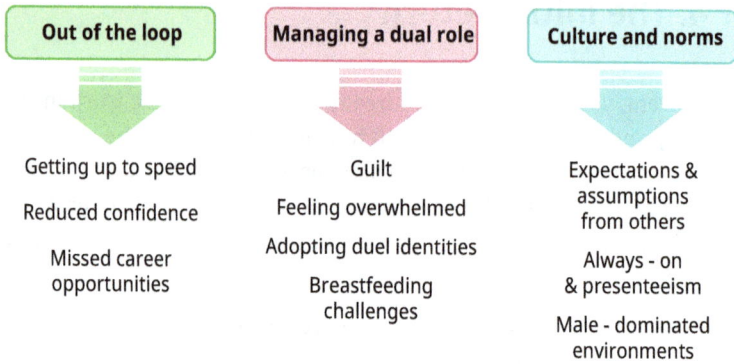

Out of the loop

Getting up to speed

Reduced confidence

Missed career
opportunities

Managing a dual role

Guilt

Feeling overwhelmed

Adopting duel identities

Breastfeeding
challenges

Culture and norms

Expectations &
assumptions
from others

Always - on
& presenteeism

Male - dominated
environments

Figure 8: Categories of challenges.

Although the strategies discussed as part of setting up for your return to work can definitely help reduce some of the potential challenges, for many returning parents it's only when the reality of being back in work and juggling both roles really kicks in, that there is an impetus to think about how to tackle these challenges. At this point the following three strategies of creating priorities and boundaries, cognitive coping, and reaching out are good to be armed with.

The returner's perspective

Creating priorities and boundaries

Many of the returners I have interviewed or coached have talked about how the ability to understand what was important to them allowed them to create priorities and boundaries between work and home and achieve a balance that felt right for them.

"Before I was so career driven, whereas now, and this initially was quite hard for me to get my head around, now I have a work life and a home life."

Creating boundaries allows returners to help manage the challenge of feeling overwhelmed and also any potential guilt around struggling to feel both a good parent and a good professional. Areas that returners decide to consider as part of their boundary setting include: what is an acceptable level of travel, deciding to turn off emails when at home, leaving on time for nursery pick-ups, and focusing on their child when at home and awake, rather than getting distracted with work.

"I was very clear about my boundary for my pick-up time, which was just a real agreement that I made with myself."

To be able to achieve a balance between home life and work, those returning from parental leave often find they naturally increase their productivity rate, are able to focus more and reduce their procrastination:

"As a group of returning mums, we're militant about how we get our work done."

"I might only be working three days but trust me you're going to get a five-day job out of me."

"I'm much more productive since I've come back. You just don't have that time for standing by the coffee machine chatting. Get in, make those decisions, get out."

Recognising that your efficiency and productivity may well have increased is a useful way of helping to alleviate any potential guilt you may be feeling about your commitment to work – a common area of guilt that returning parents feel is that they aren't delivering in the same way at work because they now have dual commitments. This increase in productivity seen in parental returners ties in with numerous studies[39,40] looking at organisations that have adopted four-day working weeks. These studies show increases in productivity as employees became more focused, along with benefits to well-being and staff retention.

As part of priority setting, it's helpful to consider how you can carve out time for yourself, and also time for you and your partner together, if you have one. Allocating this time can often be the thing that falls by the wayside, but prioritising small slots of time for yourself is great for helping to reenergise.

Some of your priorities and boundaries may change as you settle back into the workplace and have adjusted to the dual responsibilities and identities of being a working parent; there is more in *Chapter 6: Moving forwards* on how to manage working parenthood including your priorities, on an ongoing basis.

Returning after a short maternity leave

As detailed in *Chapter 2: Setting up to leave*, the average length of maternity leave in the UK is nine months, whilst in the U.S. it is 10 weeks. There are variations in other countries with much longer maternity leaves in Scandinavian countries, such as Sweden whilst others such as Bahrain and UAE also have shorter maternity leaves.[36]

Research[37] shows that those taking maternity leave of less than 12 weeks can have an increased risk of experiencing postpartum (postnatal) depression, with the researchers exploring how this is related to an increased sense of feeling overwhelmed. If you return after a relatively short maternity leave then you can experience greater challenges in trying to juggle work, whilst still undergoing the physical and emotional changes that come with giving birth and the first weeks of motherhood.

This ties into my experiences of working with mothers who take a variety of lengths of maternity leave, with those taking shorter leaves being more likely to experience a sense of guilt, experiencing greater breastfeeding challenges and feeling more overwhelmed. However, being out for a shorter period of time means that there is a reduced risk of feeling out of the loop, and a variety of research[38] indicates that for those taking longer leave (greater than six months), there is a greater risk of negative career outcomes e.g. impacts on wages and employability.

Whatever length of maternity leave you take though, what can have the greatest impact is a sense of dissonance – taking a decision that feels at odds with what is important to you. There is more in the next section on *Cognitive coping* that helps think through decision making.

Cognitive coping

There are a number of mental strategies you can adopt for coping with stressful situations, what psychologists call cognitive coping. Changing the way you think about a situation can change the way you feel, and how well you believe you can cope. The previous chapter looked at three strategies for handling common emotions: doing a reality check on your concerns; managing expectations; and emotionally preparing to leave your baby. Three additional strategies that can be used when returning into the workplace are practising acceptance, recognising strengths and rationalising decisions.

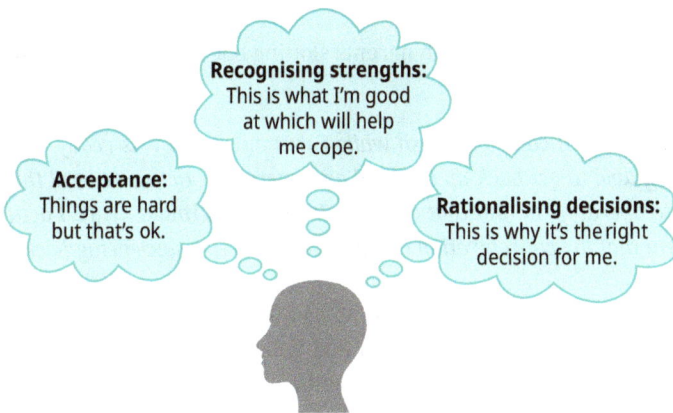

Recognising strengths: This is what I'm good at which will help me cope.

Acceptance: Things are hard but that's ok.

Rationalising decisions: This is why it's the right decision for me.

Figure 9: Cognitive coping.

Practising acceptance is a technique that involves recognising that returning to work is a challenge and there will be tough days but rather than trying to deny or avoid these feelings, which can actually cause additional stress, acknowledge and accept them.

> *"Bad days happen, you know, and you just have to accept it and move on."*

> *"That whole mantra, that it's okay to not be okay, is like a dream for me in terms of comfort. That permission from me, for it not to be okay has been huge, absolutely huge."*

Although this is easier said than done, from parents I've worked with or spoken to, those that have managed to adopt some sense of acceptance, have found it really useful. This forms part of a broader area of psychotherapy called Acceptance and Commitment Therapy (ACT), which was originally developed by a U.S.

psychologist, Steven C. Hayes in the 1980s,[41] and is widely used within the NHS currently.[42] If it's an area you'd like to explore in more detail there are some great resources that explain how to practise this technique, such as Russ Harris's *ACT made Simple.*[43]

The second coping strategy, recognising strengths, is helpful if your confidence has taken a knock. Returning after a period of absence can dent a parent's confidence, with concerns about how they are going to perform back in the workplace.

> *"I didn't feel very competent in myself, for the last year I was changing nappies and now I'm coming back into this nine-to-five role. I had anxiety about am I as good as I was before?"*

For many this concern is short lived, with parents slotting back into their working life relatively quickly.

> *"My brain had gone to a complete mush while I was out, and I was really worried about being able to get back up to speed and operate at the same level that I'd been used to operating at. But that came back virtually straight away. I actually weirdly find that my concentration and my focus is better since being back."*

However, if you are feeling you need a confidence boost when you return, it's worth taking time to reflect on your strengths and what you are good at. There are many skills that are strengthened whilst at home on parental leave whether that's time management, getting organised, diplomacy, patience, resilience or a myriad of other different skills.

> *"Being off on leave with my little one has made me have to be super patient, and actually that's something I can really use back in the office."*

The YouTube clip showing the spoof job interviews[44] for a U.S. "Director of Operations" (aka a mother) provides a humorous summary of the skills you develop whilst parenting. There are also many strengths and skills that you previously had, which are still valid and worth reminding yourself of, even if you've been out of the workplace for a while.

The final area of cognitive coping is considering how you rationalise the decisions you make. One of the traps parents can fall into is comparing themselves to others, the *compare and despair* trap as psychotherapists call it, and this comparison can mean you doubt the decisions you've made. For example, this was some of my initial thinking when deciding when and how to go back to work.

"I'm only taking six months maternity leave whereas others in my baby group are taking nine months, am I abandoning Rebecca too early? Also, should I really be going back four days a week, are they going to be taking me seriously if I'm not full-time? And how about my friends that are only working three days, does that mean I'm not as good a parent as them as I'm choosing to work longer hours?"

Other areas where comparisons are often made are decisions about childcare, decisions about career path and what role to take, decisions on working hours and when to arrive and leave, as well as all the decisions connected to a child's wellbeing such as when and how to wean. The more comparing you do the more likely you are to be unhappy with your decisions. Psychologists[45] recognise that when you have more options to choose from, then you are likely to be less satisfied with your choices as there are more possibilities to think "should I have taken that different option?".

When coaching returning parents, there are five questions that working mums and dads have found helpful to think through to help with their decision-making:

- What's best for me and my family?
- Which opinions are important to me?
- Who am I connected into?
- How can I reframe this decision?
- How long-term is this decision?

Let's look at each of these questions in turn. Firstly, rather than making decisions based on what's best for you and your family, the cultural norms and expectations within your workplace and broader society can make you feel under pressure to decide in a certain way. For example, you may be experiencing a culture that feels less accepting of part-time working or judges people based on how long they are sat at their desk. Taking a step back and really thinking through what's most important for you and your family, can help the decision-making process, considering: *Am I making this decision because I think that's the "acceptable" decision to make or actually does that not really fit with what I think is best for me and my family?*

Connected to this is deciding whose opinions and feedback are important to you. For example, it may be that you're feeling judged by your peers at work because of your working patterns, or because you are choosing to leave at a certain time.

"When I'm in the office my commute means I have to leave at 4.30, and for a lot of us that's like the middle of the afternoon; when I come in the next day there are often comments around how they were there until seven or later."

As highlighted in the last chapter (*The cultural challenges for fathers*), this is often more acutely felt for dads who have adopted "non-standard" working patterns, particularly if they are in organisations or geographies where there are strong cultural norms around how fathers should be combining work and parenting. Cultural assumptions and judgements from those closest to you can often be the hardest to manage.

> "I know that my mother-in-law doesn't approve of me working, because she gave up when she had her children, but she doesn't recognise that things are different now."

Determining whose opinions you want to pay attention to helps deflect any sense of judgement. There will always be differing opinions on how you are balancing family and career and how you are bringing up your children; it's worth stopping and thinking about whether those are the opinions you want to be paying attention to. The great quote from Eleanor Roosevelt is a useful reminder: *"Nobody can make you feel inferior without your consent."*

The third area to consider as part of your decision-making is who you are connecting into and comparing yourself with. Connecting with other working parents who have made similar decisions to you helps reduce the levels of compare and despair. For example, if you're in a full-time, full-on role, you're bound to feel more levels of guilt if you compare yourself to those working three-day weeks, being worried that you're not spending enough time with your child. Similarly, those I've coached who have decided to work more flexibly are more likely to have concerns about whether they're letting their career take a side-step if they compare themselves to others who appear to have stepped back onto the corporate fast-track.

> "It's hard to find other working dads that have taken similar decisions to me [taking shared parental leave], and although I know it's the right decision, I do feel a bit concerned sometimes when I talk to others whose careers seem to be flying."

Whatever decision you have taken, if you still have any potential doubts, then consider how you can reframe or justify to yourself to help overcome these doubts.

> "Initially I felt really selfish going back to work, but it didn't actually take me long to realise that he loves the nursery, his development has soared dramatically."

> "After a lot of soul searching and thinking I decided to accept the role that I'm in now because although it's a sidewise move, it gives me the flexibility I want, and I thought it would be another string to my bow."

Another example is a returning parent I was recently coaching who was worried about the decision they had taken to go for a promotion, which meant that they were spending more nights away from home. They had a lot of judgement from their mother who thought they shouldn't be "abandoning" their children – the way they reframed it was by thinking about the role modelling they were setting up for other working mums in their organisation and also for her own girls when they grew up. Although it's useful to have a clear process for decision-making, once the decision is made it's more helpful to think: "How do I make this decision right" rather than "Is this the right decision".

The final question to consider is "How long term is this?". For most people, the decisions you're making around returning and the different working patterns you adopt are actually only a relatively small part of your overall career. Depending on your retirement plans (which for most are a long way in the future), if you think of the total amount of time from the start of your career to the finish, the decisions you are making during this current child intensive time occupies a relatively small percentage of your overall career timeline.

Start career   Finish career

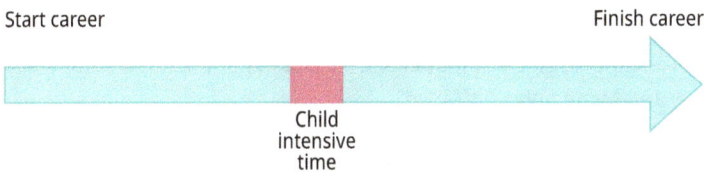

Child
intensive
time

Figure 10: Career timeline.

It can feel like the decisions you are currently making are going to impact the rest of your career, and although it's worth acknowledging in some cultures taking what can feel like a career sidestep or pause, can make an impact, there are thankfully lots of great examples out there where that isn't, or doesn't need to be, the case.

Reaching out

Sometimes when managing the transition back into the workplace, returning parents are reluctant to reach out for help as they can view it as a sign of weakness, and they may not want to admit to others that they are finding it tricky.

"I really worked myself up about not having anywhere to breast pump at work, but I didn't say anything, and just kind of overcame it – I stopped my breastfeeding journey before I really wanted to."

> *"When I was meeting up 1:1 with my team [as I returned to work], I probably didn't admit that I was finding it quite hard. I think they could see what I was going through, but because they didn't hear it from me, that didn't allow me get the type of support from them that would have been helpful."*

Rather than seeing it as a weakness, proactively asking for support, whether that's from family and friends, or within the workplace, can be seen as a sign of strength. Instead of feeling that you need to struggle on and pretend everything's ok it can show courage to speak up.

> *"My boss suggested that I showed a bit more vulnerability with the team, and I did then start to say the things I found tricky; if I'd have done that in the previous 1:1s I'd had with them I think it would be quite different."*

> *"When I came back after my second baby I had more frequent meetings with my manager. I was a bit more assertive, and asked for that, because I recognised that I needed that support."*

There are two main types of support we can reach out to others for when returning from work: emotional support and practical support. Emotional support is when you have someone to share common stories and experiences with, having a sympathetic ear, and being able to off-load.

> *"Talking to my husband helped. So, when I was getting stressed and feeling that things weren't working, I just told him and that definitely helped. I think if I had kept it bottled up, it would have just got worse and worse."*

Practical support is the hands-on help from others where they physically do things for you or provide practical assistance or information.

> *"My manager arranged some catch-up meetings with some of the new people in the team during my first week back which was helpful in getting me up to speed and connecting me in."*

When things are getting challenging, consider what type of support you're looking for and therefore who is the best person or group to reach out to, whether that's within or outside the workplace.

As part of reaching out it's also helpful to think through your working from home (WFH) patterns, if that's applicable in your workplace. Whilst WFH can provide some great flexibility, it can make it harder to reach out for help and get back up to speed if you're not seeing people face to face. Many returners I've talked to have looked to go into their workplace a bit more when they first return so they can build those connections and support networks back up. (There is more on WFH in *Managing working parenthood* in *Chapter 6*).

Support and expectations from your partner

One of the exercises I regularly do with parents, as part of both planning to go on parental leave and also as they return to work, is thinking through the expectations the working parent has for both themselves but also for their partner, if they have one. Often these expectations haven't been acknowledged or verbalised, leading to assumptions from new parents on what they are expecting their partner to intuitively pick up. For a working couple, before they have their first child, the tasks and labour at home will have been split in a certain way. If one of the couple is then off for an extended period with the baby, it's often the case that they pick up the majority of the household chores and more of the work associated with the baby. As you start to transition back into work it's really helpful to talk through how some of those practical tasks are going to be handled and what kind of support you're looking for from your partner.

> *"When I was on mat leave I let my husband sleep through the nights and didn't wake him for night feeds. I pretty much did everything at home and with our daughter because he was working full time and I wasn't. I still recall the night before I went back to work discussing with him that I needed him to start sharing more of the tasks relating to her and the home. When I woke him up to burp our daughter at 1am after I'd fed her so I could go back to sleep the day before I went back to work he did look a bit surprised. If I hadn't agreed with him who did what now I was back to work and I'd kept trying to do everything the same as I did on mat leave, I would have drowned."*

Having talked through the experiences and strategies for the returning parent, as with previous chapters, let's now consider the manager's perspective.

Manager's perspective

Although for those off on parental leave it feels like a significant change has taken place, and they can feel out of touch with the workplace, as a manager you can have a quite different perspective.

> *"Although they've been off for nine months, it hardly feels like they've been away."*

> *"It doesn't feel like much has changed in the last year they've been off."*

It can also be hard to understand the experiences that the returning parent is going through, either because you're not a parent yourself, you didn't take a period of parental leave, or it was a long time ago and hard to remember what it was like.

Similar to the focus points in the previous chapter, to help manage the transition back to work for your returning parent, there are four areas to consider:

- Communications
- Supporting flexible working
- Empathy and advice
- Role modelling

Although the discussion areas below are based on either interviews with returning parents or through my experience of working with returners and their managers, it's important to recognise that individuals vary. Recent U.S. research from a Boston business school[46] shows how managerial support works best when it is flexible and tailored to the unique return to work experience of the individual.

Communications

In the previous chapter we explored the communications prior to the returner coming back to work, focusing on keeping them up to date, inviting them to events and discussing plans for when and how to return. Once the returning parent is back in the workplace the most useful areas of communication are frequent check-ins and providing feedback.

> *"We used to have regular chats about the work I was doing, but also how I was finding it generally. It was great that I knew that I could talk to him [my manager]."*

"We made sure to have regular check-ins, just about how workloads were going and things I was struggling with."

Feeling confident on the return to work is recognised as important in helping achieve an effective transition back and can help reduce the level of conflict parents experience in managing both their work and family. This sense of conflict can have a strong impact on whether the returning parent wants to stay or leave the workplace so is important to tackle. As a manager you can have a significant impact through the feedback you give your returner, particularly for those that may be experiencing a dent to their confidence.

"It would have helped to have more regular feedback and contact with my manager, to see how I was getting on. I'm not naturally an anxious person, but I did feel I needed that confidence boost to say, 'you are doing the right things', and I didn't feel I had that. My confidence had taken a knock, and I needed my manager to say, 'you are doing a great job, of course you are, why are you worried, we want to have you back'."

It can be easy to underestimate the potential drop in confidence that returning parents experience, particularly if they aren't verbalising their concerns, so even if your working parent appears ok confidence wise, it can be worth giving them an extra boost.

Supporting flexible working

Whilst the previous chapter discussed ways to effectively set up flexible working, once the returning parent is back in the workplace there are a number of additional areas that can help make flexible working work. Firstly, if you're not already doing so, it's helpful to think about managing outputs not hours or presenteeism for your returning parent.

"What was great was that my manager said it's kind of up to you. 'You do what you need to do to get the work done. I don't care where you do it, whether it's at home or in the office, be there for your team in the way that you can get the work done. I'm going to judge you on your outcomes, not the amount of time you're sat behind your desk'. That really helped me balance my work and family life."

If you are able to adopt this outputs-driven focus within your work environment, then it can really help you to get the best out of your working parent. Supporting flexible working and having an outputs-driven approach for not just your returning parent, but also with your wider team, can also help to tackle any perceptions of unfairness, minimising beliefs from the team that the returning parent is being given special treatment because of their home commitments.

Another area that may need to be picked up with the wider team is managing any flexibility stigma,[47] the perception that those using flexible working are less committed or productive. The earlier section *Creating priorities and boundaries* provides a good understanding of how returners can actually be more focused and productive.

The final area to consider in supporting flexible working is to keep up the communications to understand how flexible working is working, as it may be that the initial agreed work pattern needs adjusting. There are more details on supporting flexible working in *Chapter 5: Support from HR and the broader organisation*.

Empathy and advice

As described in the previous chapter, asking the returning parent directly what type of support they want from you, and interpreting how your support is received, can help you get the balance right of providing empathy and advice, but not making the returner feel that you view them as incapable. Returning from parental leave normally results in a significant period of adjustment for the returner, and if they feel that you recognise this, it will go a long way to ease any anxiety they have.

> "When I was getting my brain back into it, the support of my manager was great. Him just being open to silly questions and not getting annoyed by me asking, and being happy to chat about stuff, that was really helpful."

As part of the transition back, it's also reassuring for the returner if there is a recognition that it may take a while to settle into managing childcare and the dual responsibilities.

> "He [my manager] was very flexible and understanding with my starting and leaving hours which definitely helped whilst I got myself back into the swing of it."

> "The second time I returned I worked for a woman who had two quite young children and there was a realistic expectation and reassurance that it's not a problem if something goes wrong in the first few weeks, because it will you know, it's normal."

Role modelling

As a manager, demonstrating how you manage the balance between your work priorities and your home priorities, whether that's with children or other commitments, is a great way to help returning parents set up their own priorities and boundaries. When coming back from parental leave, returners can feel like they need to hide their home life and are unsure about how to manage potentially conflicting priorities. Strategies are given earlier in the chapter to help returners think through their priorities and create the boundaries that are right for them – as a manager demonstrating where yours are helps give them permission to create their own.

> **Visibly demonstrating priorities and flexible working**
>
> The examples below are from a returning parent working in the head office of a major UK retailer, and another returning parent working in a global investment bank. Both these parents explain how their managers and other leaders visibly demonstrate their attitude to managing priorities and flexible working.
>
> *"There's a lot of competitive presenteeism within certain parts of our organisation, so 'I sent an email at 10 o'clock last night' or whatever. Whereas my manager and I both have on our email signatures, 'if you receive an email from me out of hours it's because I'm working flexibly, please don't reply until your next working day'. She's setting that tone from the top, you know, and I'm following. And actually her boss who is the CFO, she's got three-year-old twin girls and she has it on her email signature as well because she does it, she works around them. So it's flowed down all the way; that makes a difference."*
>
> *"People in this organisation will say 'I'm going to be working from home in the morning because I've got sports day". You know, it's not hiding your home life, it's bringing it to work and making that part of who you are. Management will confidently enter a meeting late and say, "I've been to little Johnny's assembly today, but I'm here now.' I've seen that loads in the Company and I love it, I genuinely love it and think it's a good place to work as a parent."*
>
> These may seem relatively small examples but can have a big impact on those within the organisation who still have a very high commitment to work, but also want to give a priority to their home life.

Checklist

Below is a summary of the things to consider either as a returning parent or as the manager of a returning parent:

Returner's checklist	√
What boundaries do I need to develop and communicate?	
How have I carved out time for myself?	
What do I need to do to practise acceptance?	
What's my list of strengths to help me cope?	
Am I connected in with working parents who have made similar decisions to me?	
How can I reframe or rationalise the decisions I've made?	
How can I reach out for more support, both practical and emotional?	

Manager's checklist	√
What level of check-ins am I doing with my returning parent?	
Am I providing the right level of feedback?	
Am I managing outputs not hours or presenteeism?	
Have I tackled any flexibility stigma?	
Have I checked in on how flexible working is working?	
Am I providing the right level of empathy and advice?	
How can I provide the right role model of combining work and outside life?	

Chapter 5: Support from HR and the broader organisation

As previously highlighted, there are five different levels of support for those returning from parental leave: National, Organisational, Leader, Team and Self-support. Most of this book has focused on the shared responsibility of managing this transition considering *Leader* support, what the manager can do to help the parental returner, and also *Self-support* – what the returner can do to help themselves.

This chapter focuses on how to make the most of *National* support, what initiatives can be put in place for *Organisational* support, and how to make the most of *Team* support.

Figure 11: Focus on National, Organisation and Team Support.

Many organisations and People or HR teams, will have policies and practices in place to support returners through this transition, which others can learn from. However, from interviewing and coaching a variety of parental returners, even organisations with lots in place could still benefit from changes in some areas. This chapter covers:

– Why is this important – why should your organisation be paying attention to this?
– KIT, SPLIT and SPL – how can you maximise the use of these UK National benefits?
– Organisation initiatives – what are others doing to support returners and how are initiatives perceived?

https://doi.org/10.1515/9783111618456-005

- Communications – keeping returning parents up to date.
- Practical support – what are the simple things that can make a big impact?
- Supporting flexible working – how easy is it to set up and what's the cultural acceptance?
- Manager's training and guidance – how can you help managers support their returners?
- Team support – how can peers across the organisation support?
- Setting the tone – what else can be done to develop a culture that's accepting of working parents?
- Checklist – summary of areas to consider.

Why is this important?

The chances are if you've been drawn to this chapter, you're already thinking that this is a worthwhile area to explore. However, from experience, employees working in People teams, HR and roles such as diversity & inclusion, may feel they need to do some persuading within their organisation to focus more attention on this topic. This summary aims to give you evidence and strategies to talk to others and spur action.

As highlighted in *Chapter 1: Introduction*, returning from parental leave is a challenging time for working parents with the need to re-engage with the workplace, switch back onto managing their careers, manage the identity transition into a working parent, whilst balancing the needs of their family. These challenges mean a percentage of mothers either don't return to the workplace, take longer career breaks or decide to leave after returning to work. There is also very low uptake of Shared Parental Leave (SPL) in the UK[48], with the majority of eligible working fathers not taking advantage of the opportunity to be on leave with their infant.

There is a recognised gender employment gap, with lower employment rates for females and differences in pay for the same role (called the gender pay gap in OECD countries). Estimates of the economic impact of this gender employment gap are as high as £1.1 billion in lost earnings annually in the UK.[49] Recent data on the gender pay gap, from the World Economic Forum[50] shows that despite some improvements it is still an issue that needs tackling globally; Sweden, the best rated country has a gap of 8%, whilst UK is 16% and U.S. 18%.

Women's role as mothers is one of the key reasons attributed to this gap and developing family-friendly policies is increasingly recognised as a way of developing greater equality in organisations. Support given around parental leave, as part of a broader set of family-friendly policies, not only helps equality, diversity and tackling the gender pay gap in organisations, but also leads to benefits of retaining talent and maintaining the well-being of employees.

With increasing expectations of family-friendly policies from current and prospective employees, having clear benefits in this area helps attract and retain staff and enhances loyalty. More organisations are understanding the benefits of having family-friendly policies and how this helps them be an employer of choice. For example, Deloitte, which is consistently ranked in the top ten family-friendly workplaces in the U.S. has its policies clearly laid out on its career pages: https://www2.deloitte.com/uk/en/pages/careers/articles/family-friendly-policies-professional.html.

As highlighted in *Chapter 3: Setting up for return*, there are numerous challenges on returning from parental leave, ranging from lack of confidence, feeling overwhelmed, adjusting to a new identity, managing expectations and coping with guilt. These can lead to stress, burnout and impacts on physical and mental health; supporting return to work for new parents can help reduce these and increase a sense of well-being.

Good return to work experiences also impact children's well-being, with research from UNICEF,[51] highlighting the benefits that family-friendly policies can provide for the health and well-being of infants, whether that's from policies around flexible working, breastfeeding support or adequate maternity leave.

Maximising use of KIT, SPLIT and SPL

In the UK there are a number of National support mechanisms such as KIT and SPLIT[i] days for keeping in touch whilst parents are away on leave, and also Shared Parental Leave (SPL). HR and the broader organisation can play a key role in how these are used, providing guidance for both returning parents and their managers to maximise their use.

As discussed in *Chapter 3: Setting up for return*, the use of KIT or SPLIT days can have a big impact on how smooth the return to work transition is. Most organisations will have guidance or processes on how KIT and SPLIT days can be used from a legislative point, but it's also helpful to outline the benefits of doing so, and ways they can

---

i In the UK up to 10 KIT days (Keep in Touch) can be taken by those on maternity leave, whilst up to 20 SPLIT days (Shared Parental Leave in Touch) can be taken by those on Shared Parental Leave.

be utilised. If not used judicially they can end up being just a way for the returner to earn money, without really helping with their transition.

> *"I took all ten of them, it was like 'there's your job, get on', but I don't think it helped with my transition back if I'm honest, I think it just boosted my wage."*

Whereas, used effectively they've been shown[52] to help returning parents keep on top of organisational progress and decisions, speed up the process of transition back to the workplace, and help individuals manage their career. Returners have effectively used them for team events, specific meetings (particularly around strategy, planning or changes within the organisation), and also for training events or coaching sessions. It can also work well to use them to phase back into the workplace.

> *"The KIT days are brilliant, to be able to come into regional meetings or celebration events, whatever that looks like, that's important."*

In countries outside of the UK, which don't have a National system of KIT days, staying in touch programmes have been implemented in organisations with clear benefits. For example, research in Canada[53] shows that keeping in touch programmes can help increase perceptions of a mother's commitment and agency.

Another National support mechanism in the UK is Shared Parental Leave (SPL), however, it's recognised that the uptake is exceptionally low, with research[54] suggesting only 1-2% of eligible couples take advantage of SPL, due to both financial and cultural barriers. Although some organisations are leading the field and providing parity for fathers taking leave, most organisations don't provide the same benefits. For those that do take SPL, this not only benefits the fathers themselves and the father-child relationship but is recognised as one of the most helpful supports for mothers.

> *"I found the most helpful support was taking shared parental leave, without a shadow of doubt. I think from an organisational perspective, the most important thing that an organisation can do is encourage their male employees to consider taking that time. Because it really makes a huge difference for the mum coming back to be able to go in and get back on their feet without worrying about that childcare piece."*

In many organisations there can be a lack of clarity on how to use SPL and it is not actively championed within the organisation. Sharing examples of those who have taken this approach can both provide role models, and help others navigate the challenges and potential barriers.

Encouraging the use of leave for fathers

Although research from the Fatherhood Institute[55] and others shows clear benefits for both the family and the organisation, when fathers take parental leave, there are barriers to uptake. One of the strongest barriers is financial, with a greater proportion of fathers being the primary earner, making it more difficult to manage financially if they take significant periods of leave.

The amount of paid leave reserved for fathers varies widely between countries, with data across OECD countries[56] showing huge differences in government policy, with Japan being one of the most generous, 52 weeks at an average of 61% pay, Slovak Republic with 28 weeks at 75% pay and Spain with 16 weeks at 100% pay. In comparison the UK has just two weeks paternity leave at 18.5% pay, whilst Israel, New Zealand and United States have no paid leave reserved for fathers.

Although affordability can be a significant barrier to fathers taking parental leave, cultural barriers also play a strong role. For example, Japan with the most generous policy has an uptake of less than 8% fathers[57]. Similarly, although many countries have now introduced some form of shared parental leave, such as the UK where 50 weeks can be shared between parents, the leave is still more used by mothers.

The Nordics are often held up as countries that are trying to break the gender stereotypes around parenting, for example Sweden was the first country to make parental leave gender neutral (back in 1974) and their current policy is to allow for up to 480 days of paid parental leave shared between the parents, with a minimum of 90 days taken by each parent.

This has led to the phenomenon of "latte dads", Swedish fathers who frequent cafes with babies in-tow, and a culture where **not** taking parental leave is largely frowned upon and the question more frequently asked by dads is "How long to take?" rather than "Will I take time off?"[58]

As an organisation if you want to encourage the use of paternal leave, what can you be doing to support fathers from both a financial and cultural perspective?

Organisation initiatives

There are numerous policies and initiatives that organisations can put in place to support those going and returning from parental leave. Some of these are specific to this transition such as phased return to work, whereas others are broader family-work support policies. In reality some of these initiatives may only be financially feasible in larger corporate organisations, however, there are some great examples of cost-efficient initiatives that any organisation can implement. The range of initiatives include:

– Support networks
– Breastfeeding support
– Phased return to work
– Training & coaching
– Childcare support

Support networks

Setting up support networks is a relatively easy and cost-efficient initiative that can have a huge impact in helping the transition back to work. Connecting the returning parent with others who are in a similar position allows them to share experiences, concerns, information and coping strategies, with research[59] showing clear benefits of working mothers having conversations with those in similar positions. In practice they work either through 1:1 buddy systems and/or group support and operate whilst off on parental leave, during the transition back and ongoing for working parents.

> *"We instigated a parental leave keeping in touch session to come in and network with others. It's run every six months for those on maternity or paternity leave, or those that have recently returned. This day-long session means they can find out what's been going on in the bank, they can connect with those who are already back at work with kids and understand how that works and it's also a connection in with the HR contact and diversity & inclusion team."*

Some organisations looking at broadening their support networks to also include those who have caring responsibilities for others, recognising the similar challenges for those caring for elderly or sick relatives.

Although initiatives such as buddy systems may not always be taken up by individuals, they're still important to have in place, as individuals vary in what they're looking for and it impacts the perception of the organisation as family friendly.

> *"There's a maternity buddies programme, I was offered, and I very deliberately went back and said, no thank you . . . I felt like I already had the buddies that I needed."*

"For me that was massively missing when I didn't have the support system in place. . . . it's definitely having things like a buddy, that would have really helped."

Breastfeeding support

Another relatively low-cost initiative is provision of facilities for expressing breast milk. During my research almost all of the returning mothers I spoke to faced challenges, which ties in with academic evidence[60,61] around how mothers have to cease breastfeeding early or conceal expressing in the workplace because of lack of facilities and/or lack of acceptance in the workplace. This leads to potential conflict between health recommendations on how to long to breastfeed for, and what feels ok or practically possible in the workplace.

"There's nothing to support breastfeeding, no private place in the office. Breast-feeding when my daughter was first born was extremely hard, and I'd just got going and then had to stop because I was returning to work. It was really hard and I got so upset."

Even when organisations do have dedicated spaces, I've heard a plethora of stories of the challenges mothers faced when using these. These ranged from having to navigate over cleaners' buckets to find a space in the room, removing bottles of wine for corporate events from the breastmilk fridge, being interrupted due to a lack of locks on the doors, and finally finding out that their breastmilk had been used for other employee's coffees. There is lots of online guidance on how to set up good support in this area for example, *Support for Breastfeeding in the workplace* on the U.S. CDC website: https://www.cdc.gov/breastfeeding/pdf/strategy5-support-breastfeeding_workplace.pdf.

As an organisation there is clear evidence[62] of the benefits of offering breastfeeding facilities including reduced maternal absenteeism, higher motivation levels and greater retention of returning mothers.

Phased return to work

A third type of initiative is the implementation of a phased return to work policy. Returning parents may look individually at how they phase their own return, with details give in the section *Choosing how to return* in Chapter 3, however, some organisations have a more formal policy. For example, one of my research participants worked in an organisation with a Phase back policy in place which allowed returners to have up to 12 weeks of reduced hours to adjust back into the workplace whilst still receiving full pay and benefits. Unsurprisingly this was seen as a huge benefit for the returning parent, and also seen as a benefit to the organisation as it encouraged parents to come back earlier and connect in more.

> *"We have this Phased back to work scheme, where anyone who's been on mater-nity leave is eligible for 12 weeks of phase back. You agree what that looks like with your line manager, so for example it can vary from one day for four weeks and then up it to two days, three days, whilst some people do one day a week for the full 12 weeks and then just go up to full time. It's a really, really good incen-tive. The maternity policy for the company is that we get six months full pay, and then it stops, but then after that you can choose this three months of phase back where you can work part-time. It encourages people to come back earlier than they may have originally thought but is also a great way to adjust back; it was definitely one of the most useful types of support I got."*

Parental training and coaching

A fourth area of organisational support is training and coaching, with an increasing number of organisations implementing 1:1 or group coaching sessions. Group coach-ing or training provides the benefit of connecting in with others in the same situa-tion whilst 1:1 coaching can help when participants want to talk through particular issues in more depth. For example, programmes for group sessions could be a one-day session before going off on parental leave, followed by a half day session around the time of return. Whilst 1:1 coaching is typically set up with sessions before leave, during leave and shortly after returning, with three to six sessions in total.

Both research[63,64] and through my own experience working in this field, coaching shows clear benefits in helping overcome return to work challenges such as guilt, lack of confidence and managing dual roles. If this is a path you wanted to follow then word-of-mouth recommendations and using providers that are accredited, for example, through ICF (International Coaching Federation) is a good place to start. Or get in contact through kirstie@blueacornsolutions.com. Alternatively, if you wanted to run the coaching in-house, there is comprehensive guidance on setting up internal mentors for new parents from Seignot & Clutterbuck's *Mentor-ing New Parents at Work*[65].

Childcare support

The final type of initiative is childcare support, whether that's providing an onsite nursery or more commonly giving a provision of emergency childcare for when a working parent isn't able to use their regular childcare, for example, if their child is ill and can't go into nursery. Although these do provide a clear benefit to the returning parent, in practice they're not always as well received as you might expect.

"We have a nursery on-site which has slightly reduced rates compared to a regular nursery, it's great that it's so convenient, however, in practice it's really hard to get a space there, the waiting list is over a year."

"We have an emergency childcare back up, with six sessions of four hours every year, which translates to three days. Although that feels really good, in reality what you end up doing is thinking, well is she sick enough that we use one, or do we just try and mosey through. I just think it's nonsense. If they said that they're unlimited or for example, 20 days, I think it would be worth their while as it's much better that they get even half a workday than not getting anything from me [because I'm having to care for an ill child]."

If you currently have a policy around childcare support or are looking to implement one, it's worth considering whether there needs to be adjustments to make sure the investment is providing the benefits you were expecting.

Which initiatives to implement?

When deciding which initiatives to propose, encourage or put in place within your organisation, it's worth considering research[66] that shows that having a range of different initiatives in place results in increased job satisfaction and job commitment. A wider range of family-friendly initiatives also increases the likelihood of people making use of the policies. However, this is off-set by the perceptions of how family-supportive the organisation is, having the benefits or policies alone is not enough if the organisation isn't seen as family-friendly. Whilst deciding which initiatives to propose or implement, it's worth considering whether these will be perceived as a tick-box exercise by returning parents or whether they genuinely feel part of a supportive culture. Having a set of policies can be great, but returners also want a sense of support whether that's from HR, their manager or from others in their team.

"We have all these policies in place, HR handed me this 20-page document I had to wade through, but actually what I wanted was a bit more of the human side."

Managing parental leave in SMEs

Managing parental leave can feel more challenging in small businesses, with research from the UK government[67] indicating that within SMEs having a parent out the organisation for up to a year feels a bigger impact than for those in larger organisations. There are also greater concerns for SMEs around the uncertainty of whether an employee will return, and the financial impact can be felt more acutely.

However, research from International Labour Organisation[68] (ILO) indicates that actual costs incurred by SMEs are often less than anticipated, and many measures such as providing breastfeeding support have minimal associated costs.

The guidance and checklists within this book should provide a strong starting point to think through areas you need to consider as part of managing parental leave and pay, there are also additional checklists available online e.g. those from the UK charity Working Families.[69]

Although not a legal requirement, having policies in place around parental leave and pay (maternity, paternity and adoption) and around flexible working helps the employee be clear on the process and provides protection for the company against discrimination claims. There is a variety of guidance online from HR specialists on developing these policies.[70] Some SMEs outsource HR responsibilities, alternatively they can have someone in the organisation who takes ownership for keeping up to date with changes in parental pay and leave.

The advice is to start planning early for how to cover responsibilities whilst your employee is on parental leave and also ensure that you have mechanisms for keeping in contact, whether that's through KIT days or through informal mechanisms; UK data[71] indicates that SMEs are less likely than larger corporates to keep in contact with employees when they are off, and have a lower awareness of KIT days.

Communications

Whatever initiatives you have in place or plan to implement, I've seen in both my research and studies carried out by others, that there can be a lack of clarity or awareness of what's out there for those returning from parental leave, or more broadly what family-friendly policies the organisation has. Sadly, organisations can have some great initiatives, but they aren't always widely known about, with new parents often only hearing about them by word of mouth.

> *"I didn't realise this Managing pregnancy and beyond course was available, it would have been great to have known about it for my first pregnancy rather than only finding out now when having my second child."*

It can help if some of the information sharing happens automatically e.g. when a pregnant mother hands in her MATB1 form[ii] she gets a reminder about the support networks and in-house maternity transition training. In addition, it's helpful to think through what other communication mechanisms you can take advantage of to let people within the organisation know about the family-friendly policies you offer, whether that's team updates, newsletters etc. This communication can be directed at both those that are going to use them but also across the organisation to help set the culture of diversity and inclusion.

Thinking more broadly, if you're not already doing so, it's also helpful to publicise and communicate the support and initiatives you offer to working parents on your website and any social media platforms. In the UK the "Parental Fog Index"[72] highlights the organisations that use these channels to clearly communicate their family-friendly benefits to prospective employees. The top-rated organisations are recognised for publishing what they have in place, including details of their pay and parental leave policies, along with case studies and career progress of flexible workers. As highlighted earlier in *Why this is important*, having family-friendly policies helps your organisation be an employer of choice; visibly communicating your support for working parents is important to attract would-be employees.

---

ii A form given at 20 weeks onwards to pregnant mothers in the UK from their doctor or midwife, which is passed onto employers to show their eligibility for maternity leave.

Practical support

One of the areas that consistently came up in my research was the practical support that returners wanted. When parents return to the workplace, one of the challenges they face is the time it takes to reorientate, getting up to speed with the changes that have happened whilst they've been off. Most returners also experience a sense of feeling overwhelmed. Because of these additional pressures, it can be easy to underestimate the support that's needed. Not sorting out some of the simple practical things such as passes, phones and computer access can have a big impact.

> *"The chances are your system didn't work, your phone didn't work. You know, the basics were a bit crap . . . It's basic stuff that when you're in treacle it sticks, and it feels overwhelming. Whereas if you said to me now your phone number has been reallocated I'd be annoyed but could easily sort it."*

When employees are out of the systems or workplace for a significant chunk of time, it can take a while to re-orientate. In my research and 1:1 coaching it varies from three to six months to adjust back into the workplace. One helpful way of viewing returners is to apply some of the same principles and processes for new people entering the organisation.

> *"So, coming back into the fold it was like, I felt like the newbie yet again, and I felt like I had to start from scratch . . . it was like basically being a new person again."*

> *"There was a lot of changes when I got back. There was a lot of new people that I didn't know, but I felt like I was the new person coming in even though I had been there years and years."*

> *"You were plonked back at your desk to carry on, and obviously for me I wasn't gone that long [six months], but you know it's still not like a two-week holiday, so catching up on things can be quite hard if you're not told everything."*

What can be really helpful for returning employees is a returners' induction pack outlining the changes that have taken place, both in the industry but also within the organisation. In practice this could be a standard pack which is then adapted by different departments or divisions. Returners talk about having to wade through thousands of emails to try and find the relevant information of what has changed so packaging up this information can be a massive help and reduce rework. This can also be done through a buddy system with someone allocated to get them up to speed.

Even if the employee is out of the workplace for a relatively short period of time, for example if you're based in a geography where there is typically much shorter parental leave (e.g. an average of 10 weeks in the U.S.) there can still be significant changes that have taken place.

In addition, if not already in place, those going on parental leave and returning to the workplace need clear guidance on pay, holidays, maternity leave etc, and what their responsibilities are for keeping the organisation informed.

"When I was going off on leave I didn't know whether I had to put my plans formally in writing or whether it was acceptable to hold them verbally with my line manager. It would have been helpful to have that clarity."

"There was a return policy, but it wasn't particularly clear and there was lots of ambiguity in some of it. It unfortunately led to a bit of confusion on both sides, and it created tension, like how could I use my accrued holiday. It ended up in this very kind of hostile negotiation as it wasn't clear in the policy."

Supporting flexible working

The ability to work flexibly within an organisation can have a massive impact on the sense of well-being and loyalty to the organisation.

"Being able to come back part-time is what has helped me most to transition back. I'm not saying I'll never go back full-time because I potentially will, but it's been great having this time with him [my son] because I'll never get it back."

"They were good with the fact that I came back part-time, there's not many businesses like ours that have let people do that and they have to be respected for that."

It may be worth considering the organisation's processes and procedures to set up part-time or flex working. How this works gives a clear message to employees on whether flexible working really is accepted. Within organisations the processes to set up flexible working can cause an added stress or can be seen as supportive.

"I decided to formalise a flexible working arrangement and make a formal request. That was a horrifically painful process; I'm sure they did it to deter people."

"They were pretty good to be fair. I requested what I was looking for and they accepted straight away, so there wasn't any sort of toing and froing."

On a broader level it's worth considering how flexible working is accepted within the organisation and how it's managed on a day-to-day basis. Lots of this will be down to individual managers, but it's worth considering what can be changed culturally to make it acceptable.

> *"The company have been amazing. If I ever text them and she's not well or I need to go and pick her up, it's just 'yes go, don't worry about it.' It's not been said openly, but it's kind of take as much time as you need, it's not a problem. Whenever I've needed time off to leave early, or arrive late for whatever reason, nothing has ever been said, which is very comforting when you talk to other people, and it is a problem at their work. They know that at night when she's in bed I will get my laptop out and I will do things, but you want to do that because they're so good with me."*

The benefits and implementation of flexible working

Returning from parental leave is one of the key times that employees look to adjust their working patterns and work more flexibly. A large volume of research e.g. from the Chartered Institute of Personnel and Development (CIPD)[73] highlights the benefits of enabling flexible working within organisations, ranging from the ability to recruit and retain a broader more diverse pool of talent; increased employee engagement, motivation and productivity; reduction of work-related stress and staff absenteeism; and also the ability to be more responsive and adaptable to customer demands. A variety of studies[74] in different countries have also highlighted the well-being and productivity benefits of working a four-day work week, with trials held by Microsoft, Uniqlo, and the Icelandic government amongst others.

A recent report from the UK based CIPD[75] provides great insights on how to enable flexible working. Using research and best-practice examples from a broad cross-section of organisations, the key recommendations to consider are:

- Highlight the management benefits of flexible working, focusing on the areas that are particularly applicable in the organisational context e.g. retention, gender pay gap, diversity.
- Think more broadly about the different range of flexible working practices that could be implemented within the organisation, including the use of pilots to measure and evaluate different options.
- Develop flexible working practices for recruiting, developing and appraising employees, considering how roles can be done flexibly from the start, and how employees who are working flexibly can still develop their career and be fairly appraised.

- Share success stories and provide specific support to get the buy-in from line managers. This could include support with job design, sharing learnings from implementation in other parts of the business and overcoming resistance to flexible working.

Manager's training and guidance

All of the areas covered so far have been focused on the returner themselves, and how best to support them, one of the final areas to consider is what support would be helpful for the managers of those returning from parental leave. It's recognised that managers play a critical role in helping the transition back into the workplace and returners within the same organisation can have a very different experience depending on who their manager is.

Giving managers a greater awareness of the different experiences of parental returners can help them in turn provide the right level of support. Typical areas that would be covered in awareness training include understanding the challenges, thinking through ways to support returners, and how to help the returner to help themselves. An advantage of doing this in a group setting e.g. a half day workshop, is that they can then also compare their experiences of managing returners with others.

One area to include within training for managers is equipping them to have honest two-way conversations with their parental returner, openly discussing what the individual wants and needs and what is possible and not possible. These conversations need to be ongoing as things are likely to change from both the individual's and the organisation's perspective.

Managers I've spoken to have also appreciated, or sought, details around what's in place from an organisational perspective for those going on and returning from parental leave. This includes:

- An understanding of the policies connected with maternity, paternity and adoption leave and return.
- Clarity around what their role is in the process i.e. which responsibilities sit with them and which sit with HR.
- Information on the support available from an organisation perspective, e.g. training or buddy networks, so that they can share this information with their returners.

Team support

Most of this chapter has focused on *National* and *Organisational* support, the final area to consider as part of broader support is *Team* support – how co-workers, peers and others in the organisation can support returning parents.

Depending on the life stage and life choices of the parental returner's peer group, there can be a lack of understanding from others which can make it harder for the returner.

> *"My responsibilities are so different now. I think members of the team sort of saw that and were a bit judgmental about my shift in priorities. There was very little understanding from the team about what I might be going through."*

> *"A lot of the team are younger, so for them it's not really in their ballgame [understanding parenthood], they're, you know, just enjoying life. But thankfully my manager was really supportive, so that was ok."*

Whereas when there is understanding and empathy it can have a big impact, with studies showing that support from the wider group and co-workers can help reduce the turnover for maternity returners[76]. Having a shared understanding and empathy from others around the challenges of juggling dual roles, tiredness, feeling guilty and shifting priorities can help normalise emotions for those returning from parental leave and help them manage the transition more smoothly.

> *"That empathy that I got, that understanding and feeling like people that I spoke to had been there and that it was normal, and it's okay to feel like that, I think that really helped. Because then I just saw it kind of logically as okay, it's really hard, but, okay, this is just a process I need to get through."*

As well as providing emotional support to help returners through the transition, co-workers can demonstrate support through more practical ways, such as sharing resources and knowledge, helping other working parents adjust their work and proactively help develop solutions[77].

The support networks previously mentioned can be one of the most useful ways of encouraging this support from peers whether that's one-to-one or in a group setting. As well as this support from those who have been in similar positions, encouraging the broader organisation to show understanding is also useful, for example introducing awareness training or communication similar to that previously mentioned for managers.

Setting the tone

The beginning of this chapter outlines why this is an important area and has then given lots of details of initiatives to put in place, training and guidance and how to support flexible working. However, as highlighted earlier, if the organisation isn't perceived as family-supportive then despite having a whole range of potential policies and initiatives it can feel like a tick-box exercise. In reality, it is the tone that the organisation sets that will really make the difference.

What is the attitude and tone set by managers and colleagues during pregnancy, during leave and on return? What actually happens when a pregnant individual asks for a seat in a standing meeting? What actually happens when an individual comes in late because they've been throwing up with morning sickness, and what actually happens when a parent can't work because their child is sick? Do the line managers and others roll their eyes and sigh deeply, do they have muttered conversations about what they really think about these inconveniences, or do they genuinely offer support?

How as an organisation can you set a tone that being pregnant, taking parental leave or working flexibly isn't a "problem" that the individual should feel guilty about, but rather the organisation recognises and includes those that are working parents? One clear way of doing this is using senior managers to role model and share their experiences of going on leave, returning and then juggling work and childcare. If this becomes part of regular and "ok" conversations to have then others are likely to follow their lead and feel more comfortable.

> *"Our CEO is the main carer for his daughter, and he's very open about the fact that that's his world, that's his priority and yet he's still running a huge organisation. He talks about how he juggles during our company meetings and that flows down through the organisation."*

Checklist

Below is a summary of the areas that you may want to consider for helping support those returning from parental leave.

Checklist	√
What do we need to do to inform the organisation about the importance of supporting parental returners?	
How can we help returners maximise the use of KIT and SPLIT days, and SPL – what guidance can we give?	
What other organisation initiatives should we bolster or considering putting in place? E.g. support networks, breastfeeding support, phased return to work, parental coaching and training, childcare support, support for managers	
How are we communicating our family-friendly policies and initiatives both internally and externally?	
How are working parents practically supported on return, and is some type of returners induction needed?	
Do we need to do anything to increase the acceptance of flexible working and how easy is the process?	
What could we be doing to support the managers of those returning from parental leave?	
What else do we need to do to encourage support from the wider organisation and peers?	
What else do we need to do to set the right tone, encourage role modelling and sharing of experiences?	

Chapter 6: Moving forwards

As discussed back in *Chapter 3: Setting up for return*, when we looked at the challenges of returning to work, it typically takes three to four months to adjust back, with some returning parents feeling it takes as much as six months to fully transition into balancing their dual roles of parent and professional. This final chapter is the opportunity, once you have adjusted back into the workplace, to consider how you want to manage working parenthood on an ongoing basis and as a manager, how you can continue to support working parents. There are also strategies to manage your working patterns whatever your home circumstances.

This chapter covers:

– Returner's perspective – providing support for others, managing your career, returning a second time.
– Manager's perspective – managing stereotypes and biases, supporting career progression.
– Broader strategies to manage the balance – working from home, managing boundaries, time management techniques.

Returner's perspective

Providing support for others

Having transitioned and settled back into the workplace, many returning parents have a desire to help support other returners. Initiating changes and providing feedback to help other returning parents can provide you with a sense of achievement and of giving back. If you have had a poor experience on returning to work, it can also bring a sense of resolution by helping you feel that you have been proactive and taken some steps to bring about changes.

> *"I spent a lot of time sitting down with HR and explaining my experience, what I went through and giving suggestions to help others. I found that that helped me feel better about what I went through."*

> *"I've got a lady in my team who's just returned from mat leave, and I've made sure that she has had the experience that she wants, not the experience I had."*

> *"After my experience I've set up a support network, it's not official yet, but I'm trying to set up 'mummyships' between colleagues. I think there should be the*

https://doi.org/10.1515/9783111618456-006

opportunity to help new mums understand how to cope and recognise there's light [at the end of the tunnel]. It's through conversation that you get confidence."

There are a number of areas where returning parents have helped others, including: taking the learnings from their parental return to ensure that any returners in their team have a good experience; setting up buddy networks to help connect in newly returned parents; setting up training or information days for parents before they return to work and finally carrying out reviews with HR on how policies and communication can be updated and improved.

Reciprocity and self-efficacy – How supporting others helps yourself

The term "self-efficacy", originally coined by Stanford psychology professor Albert Bandura back in the 70s[78], means how much individuals believe they have the ability to take action, make changes or succeed. Having self-efficacy beliefs means someone is more likely to persist when faced with difficulties or challenges and is more able to implement coping strategies.

Although it's helpful to have a sense of self-efficacy, research[79] has shown that if an individual receives support from others, it can reduce their self-efficacy beliefs – they start to doubt their ability to help themselves and cope with the difficulties they are facing. However, if there is a degree of reciprocity, where individuals balance receiving support with also providing support to others then then their self-efficacy beliefs can be bolstered back up again, a sense of "I'm ok to get help as long as I'm also helping others".

What's interesting is how this applies to returning mothers – does receiving support impact my self-efficacy beliefs differently depending on how long ago I came back from maternity leave? Reciprocity research carried out with almost 300 returning mothers[80] looked at how they felt about the balance of support they were receiving and offered others, at different time periods after returning to work. When mothers first returned, (data collected five weeks after returning), the research showed that receiving more support than they offered to others was beneficial for the returning mothers and helped with the transition back. This early stage of transition back after maternity leave is recognised as having significant demands and challenges, and therefore receiving a high level of support, compared to offering support to others, is viewed as helpful and acceptable by both the individual and by others. This imbalance, called "over-benefiting", is beneficial as it doesn't impact the returning mother's sense of self-efficacy and they still feel able to implement their own coping strategies.

However, the data collected at 11 weeks after returning showed there was a shift, with a negative impact if returning mothers felt there was an imbalance in support offered and received. If they felt they were over-benefiting (receiving more support than they were giving), it started to impact their levels of self-belief. This is the stage when many returning parents start to want to think about how they can then support others, to help get the balance right, and therefore increase their sense of self-efficacy.

This research shows the importance of accepting that early support from others and not feeling bad about it, and also how once the returning parent feels settled, providing support to others can help them feel more resilient and better able to cope.

Managing your career

Back in *Chapter 3: Setting up for return* there were discussions on deciding your working hours and role, as well as thinking about how you balance the three areas of fulfilment, finances and flexibility.

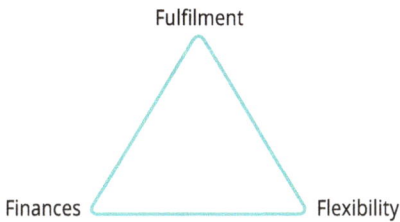

Fulfilment

Finances   Flexibility

Figure 12: Achieving the balance – the 3 Fs.

Once you have made your initial transition back into the workplace and have settled into your role as a working parent with the levels of juggling you have to do, it's often useful to take a step back and think about how the balance of these three areas is working for you and whether you want to make any adjustments. This could, for example, be considering the level of fulfilment you are getting from your current role and whether you want to adjust the type of work you're doing and the responsibilities you are taking on.

> *"Now I feel more settled I want to start taking on some more challenging work and I'm looking to do a bit more travelling."*

Sadly, there are recognised stereotypes of working mothers being viewed as less committed, reliable or career-focused compared to fathers or their child-free counterparts[81] and there are similar stereotypes for fathers that work part-time. Depending on the culture of your organisation and any biases you are experiencing, it may be that you want to make adjustments to your working pattern so that you can get the level of fulfilment that feels right for you.

> *"When I first came back I was working a three-day week which felt right at the time, however, I really feel now that I'm viewed as a second-class employee and not getting on the kinds of projects I want, so I want to go up to four days as I think I'll be taken more seriously then."*

It may be that the level of fulfilment you are getting from your work feels right, but that you want to make adjustments, based on the amount of flexibility you want and/or your financial situation.

> *"I'm finding being back full-time too much and so I'm going to have a conversation with my manager to see how I can adjust my role."*

> *"Our family finances have changed and so I want to go back up to full-time hours, I feel I can manage that ok now as our daughter has settled in really well to nursery."*

Before having discussions with your manager around any changes you want to make, it's important to talk it through with your partner, if you have one, so that you can reach an agreement as a family around what is the right balance of these three areas, fulfilment, flexibility and finances, for you as a family unit.

Notifying and returning a second time

Depending on your plans for the size of family you want, the gap you want between children, and how easily you or your partner are able to get pregnant, you may be back on the cycle of notifying work, planning to leave and then returning again. For many mothers, particularly if they have fairly recently returned, there is an anxiety about getting pregnant again and when to notify work.

"I've only been back a few months and I've just got pregnant again. I'm in a real dilemma about when to tell work – I want to be as honest as possible, but I also don't want to be written off."

"Although I'm thrilled that our next round of IVF has been successful, I'm not sure how work are going to take it and so I'm holding off telling them for now."

"This time round I seem to be showing much earlier than before and so I'm worried that everyone is going to guess I'm pregnant again."

When I'm coaching maternity returners who have become pregnant again, I'm often asked when is the right time to notify work. As with first pregnancies, the recommendation is normally to wait until the end of your first trimester as the earliest point to notify, as that is when the risk of miscarriage is reduced, whilst the latest you can notify work in the UK, is 15 weeks before your baby is due.[82] Whilst there is no right time, it can be helpful to think about whether there are any particular deadlines, projects you're about to complete, or performance reviews that are about to happen that you want to get accomplished before you talk to your manager. However, this is balanced with being as open with your employer as you feel able, helping them think about how they'll plan for your next period of absence.

There are a few tactics that can help when notifying your manager:

- *Picking a time that's better for them* – for example if you know there is a particularly stressful deadline approaching can you wait until that's passed?
- *Help them plan how to cover your work* – when you pass on your news, being proactive and sharing thoughts with your manager on how your work can be covered, will help them feel less impacted by your news.
- *Don't feel the need to apologise* – there can often be a sense of guilt attached to going off on maternity leave, particularly if your pregnancies are close together; acknowledging that it may make things trickier for your manager and your team is ok, however apologising can send an unhelpful message that you feel you've done something wrong.

As mentioned earlier, a recent maternity coachee of mine was somewhat taken aback when their manager exclaimed *"I thought you'd finished"*, when she told him about her second pregnancy. If you think that you have a manager that's going to be less accepting of your news, then it's helpful to remember that your decision to have another child doesn't need to imply that you are less committed to your job.

After going on a second, (or third or fourth) parental leave, you may, like many returning parents, find there is a shift in what you find challenging. Those returning for a second, or subsequent time, tend to have a greater understanding of what they need to make the transition as smooth as possible, but also experience a greater sense of feeling overwhelmed or tired as they also have the responsibility of caring for their older children.

> "I was much clearer the second time on what support I needed from my manager, and I was more assertive on asking for regular check-in meetings to help understand how I was getting on."

> "This time [returning for a second time] I had the experience – I allowed myself permission for it not to work well straight away and I reached out more for help and support."

> "I found I was much more tired after I'd had Hannah [my second child]. Although I knew more what I was doing, I found when I got home from work having to manage the two of them much more exhausting."

Returning a second time can also have an impact on your sense of identity, with many now feeling that they have made a shift from being a couple with a child to being a family.

> "I remember bringing my second son home from hospital and thinking 'oh, now we're a family'."

As discussed back in *Chapter 2: Preparing to leave*, research[83] shows that identity changes can impact a mother's sense of well-being. If you feel there is a mismatch between your balance of work and home life, and your sense of identity, it can increase your stress levels. You may therefore find that returning a second time you want to discuss your working patterns again.

> "When I went back the first time I was happy doing a four-day week, but I really felt that after my second child I wanted to shift the balance. I had a much stronger identity as a mother with two at home and so I talked to my manager about shifting to a three-day working week."

Manager's perspective

Having supported your working parents before they go off on leave, helped them return and supported the transition back, this final section looks at ways that you can support working parents on an ongoing basis. Many of the strategies and tactics are a continuation of those highlighted earlier in *Chapter 3: Setting up for return* and also in *Chapter 4: The initial return*. For example, thinking through communications, support for flexible working and role modelling are all still important areas. The additional areas of focus for this last *Manager's perspective* are: managing stereotypes and biases and supporting career progression.

Managing stereotypes and biases

There are a number of areas to take into consideration when managing stereotypes. In *Chapter 3: Setting up for return*, the concept of cultural norms and challenges was introduced, specifically looking at the motherhood penalty and fatherhood forfeits. To recap, mothers can be seen as less reliable, employable or competent than their child-free counterparts, experiencing the *motherhood penalty*, whilst for males, upon becoming fathers, they can be viewed more favourably, with increased promotion prospects and greater employability, known as the *fatherhood bonus*. The bias behind this discrimination is the belief that upon becoming mothers, females will put more emphasis on their family rather than their career and so be less committed, whilst for males the extra responsibility of fatherhood means stronger commitment so they can provide for their family. However, if dads shift away from the gendered norm of working full-time and being the main breadwinner, they too can experience negative biases, or *fatherhood forfeits*, being mocked, considered idle or being viewed with cynicism if they work part-time or take parental leave.

The other main area of potential stereotypes and bias is the *flexibility stigma*, initially introduced in *Chapter 4: The initial return*, with a perception that those who use flexible working are less committed or productive, whereas actually the research (detailed in *Chapter 5: Support from HR and the broader organisation*) shows clear benefits for flexible working including increased engagement, greater motivation, reduced absenteeism and decreased stress levels.

As a manager and leader within the organisation it can be useful to reflect on where you may have potential biases or perceived stereotypes around working parents and how those may be leaked to those in your team. Also reflecting on how you are role modelling acceptance of working and pregnant parents. For example, do you occasionally make throw away comments that send signals to both the individual and the wider team around how you actually view working parents? If a shift in perception and mindset is needed, then it can be helpful to read back through the benefits of flexible working in Chapter 5.

A final area to consider around stereotypes is how if they are perceived by others, then they are more likely to become true. Research looking at the career progression of working parents[84] showed that although working parents aren't actually less committed or career focused, if they experience these stereotypes from others, then it makes them feel less motivated, decreases well-being and reduces productivity compared to parents who didn't experience these stereotypes. Believing others think it, can make it come true.

Supporting career progression

Once a working parent has transitioned back into the workplace you may need to have a follow-up career discussion, helping them think through any shifts that are needed in their balance of finances, flexibility and fulfilment and what the next steps to progress their career are. Once the returning parent has been back a few months, and hopefully settled and adjusted into their pattern as a working parent, there may be changes that they want to make in how they are working. Whether that's taking on more challenging work or potentially asking to scale back and readjust their working hours. Hopefully if you are already having regular 1:1 catch-ups you are aware of how they are finding things, otherwise it's helpful to schedule in time together to talk through.

Broader strategies to manage the balance

Although the sense of feeling overwhelmed, that the majority of working parents feel when they first return to work, diminishes as the transition back into work progresses, that sense of juggling and getting the balance right continues to exist for many parents. There are three areas that are helpful to think through: working from home, setting boundaries and time management techniques. Although these areas are useful for working parents, their applicability is much broader and extends to others that have responsibilities or commitments outside of the workplace, or anyone that feels under pressure, including the managers of returning parents.

Working from home

Since the Covid pandemic that started in 2020, there has been a greater shift to working from home for many employees. Many organisations now offer a hybrid model of working with either an expectation or an agreed minimum number of days that an employee needs to be in the office, with the other days being worked from home. (This is normally either a contractual agreement or a more informal working practice). Although being home-based can provide advantages for working parents and others, there are also disadvantages. During the pandemic there was a significant increase in research[85] looking at the impacts of working from home and being aware of these can help you determine the strategies needed to get the mix of home and workplace working that's right for you.

Working from home has brought a variety of upsides or advantages for employees, but there are number of downsides also connected with this shift in how we work. The following table summarises the upsides and downside of homeworking, with further details below, including tips and techniques to overcome any potential downsides.

Table 3: Upsides and downsides of home working.

Upside	Downside
Less travel time	*but longer working hours and lack of transition*
Greater focus and concentration . . .	*but work intensification and lack of switch-off signals*
More family time . . .	*but greater work-family conflict*
Reduced hierarchy	*but online fatigue, online visibility and poorer communications*
More autonomy . . .	*but more social isolation and poorer working relationships*

One of the immediate upsides that people cite as an advantage of working from home is the reduced travel time; no longer having to commute into the workplace can free up time, reduce stress levels, with an added benefit of reduced travel costs. In practice what many find however, is that the time that they spent commuting is actually just transferred into longer working hours and that the lack of transition from home into the workplace and back again makes it harder to switch into work in the mornings and to switch off in the evenings.

A second way that home working can be useful, is that it can allow for greater focus and concentration, away from the disturbances and interruptions of the workplace. Before the pandemic this was one of the key reasons that people chose to sometimes work from home – having space without interruptions to get things done. However, with more frequent periods of working from home, that lack of interruptions or noise from others can lead to greater work intensity; people can miss the signals from others who are taking breaks, stopping for lunch or going home at the end of the day. Missing these signals can lead to lack of switching off or having down time, with setting a sustainable work pattern resting more with the individual.

If you are a working parent, the third potential upside of working from home is that you are able to spend more time with your family.

> *"Working from home has been great as I'm now able to walk my kids to school which I was never able to do before. I really appreciate having those 20 minutes with them most mornings."*

However, parents have also reported greater work-family conflict with their home life intruding on their working life making it harder to separate the two areas. This can be particularly tricky if you have younger children and/or your childcare is based in your own home.

> *"It was heart-wrenching being on a work call while my youngest was wailing outside the door. At one stage she came in and was clinging onto my leg crying whilst I was trying to maintain a professional persona."*

Overcoming these potential downsides mentioned above: longer work hours, lack of transition, work intensification, lack of switch-off signals and work-family conflict, can be overcome through boundary management, which is discussed in the next section.

The other areas of potential upsides and downsides are connected with being online and having less face-to-face contact. Working from home has meant that people are spending more time online, with face-to-face meetings or phone calls being replaced with online meetings. Although being online can have an advantage of reduced hierarchy, on a Teams or Zoom call you take up an equal space on the screen and there isn't the dynamic of going into your boss's office, research shows that spending more time online can lead to greater levels of fatigue[86] and online meetings can lead to poorer communications with lower levels of trust[87].

Similarly, although reduced face-to-face contact has led to greater autonomy and examples of employees feeling more empowered, there is clear evidence that working remotely, with the majority of communication online, has led to more social isolation and poorer working relationships. This can be particularly acute for returning parents as they have been out of the system for a while and so need to spend time building up their connections with others again.

> *"I consciously decided to go into the office more when I first returned to work, as although it made it harder doing the drop-off and pick-up at nursery, I wanted to spend that time face-to-face to reconnect back in with my colleagues."*

To help overcome these potential downsides associated with being more online and less face-to-face it's useful to think through how you can maximise your time when you are in the office to connect in with people. Proactively networking, building in time for conversations and being strategic about who you connect with helps you develop better working relationships and is particularly important if you're returning after parental leave or are new to the organisation or team.

When you meet with someone face-to-face you are more likely to spend time affinity building at the beginning of the conversation, for example by asking about their weekend, whereas when you are online, you are more likely to get quickly "down to business". Losing this affinity building means there is less trust, reciprocity and poorer working relationships. Some managers are actively thinking about how to overcome this challenge through building in this connection time during online meetings or phone conversations.

> *"Since we've been having our team meetings online, I have consciously built in time at the beginning of the meeting to allow people to connect in with each other."*

Others are using processes such as Reciprocity Rings[88], where participants actively think about how they can support each other – putting forward micro-requests for where they want help, and then others responding on where they can help or give input. (For more details on Reciprocity Rings see Adam Grant's book *Give and Take*[89]).

Managing boundaries

Back in *Chapter 4: The initial return*, we discussed the importance of creating priorities and boundaries as a returning parent. For both working parents and others, having boundaries between home and work life is important to allow you to more easily switch off. If you don't have the ability to switch off then you are more likely to experience increased stress levels and burn-out.[90]

If you are working from home consistently, rather than the odd day here or there, the need for creating boundaries becomes more acute. Previously, employees who weren't working from home had both temporal and spatial segregation – time at work and time at home and a separate work space and home space. With the increase of working from home, work life and home life have become intertwined in an unprecedented way.

There are three types of tactics you can use to create boundaries when home working – having physical boundaries, time-related actions and setting up boundary behaviours.

Where possible creating a physical boundary between your work space and living space can help reduce stress. Research has shown that workers have reduced stress levels if they are able have a room which they primarily use for work, with a door that they can close at the end of the workday.[91] In practice this isn't possible for many people and therefore if you aren't able to use a spare bedroom or be lucky enough to have a home office, then having a separate desk in the corner of the room can help create that boundary, rather than using the kitchen table. Whichever table you're using, if you don't have a separate room for working, it's also helpful to clear you work stuff away and avoid using your relaxing space as a work space.

> *"I found that I was using my sofa to sometimes take work calls but then in the evenings when I was sitting back on the sofa it took me back into a work headspace. After learning about creating physical boundaries I found it much better to keep my calls in my work space at home, otherwise I found it harder to switch off."*

Time-related actions that can help create boundaries and reduce work intensification include setting start and finish times for yourself, taking lunch breaks and blocking time out in your diary. Depending on the culture and acceptance within your organisation it's also helpful to get outside for a walk or other exercise during the day.

> *"I really encourage my team to get out for a walk at some stage during the day, I've found that if they take that short break they are actually much more efficient for the rest of the day and by showing that I trust them to not*

abuse working from home, I've actually found that it increases their commitment to the organisation."

Other boundary behaviours that people have found helpful to adopt include creating a fake commute, maintaining the same work attire as worn in the office and purposefully disconnecting, such as choosing times to silence messages or turn off your phone.

"I found it really helpful to have a fake commute where I leave my house and go for a 10-minute walk around the block and then re-enter with my work mindset on."

Whether working from home or not, the other useful technique for managing boundaries is communicating your boundaries to others, setting expectations with your colleagues and confronting those who violate your boundaries. In practice this involves being clear on what your work patterns are, whilst still recognising the need to be flexible.

"When they asked me to come to a regular 8.00 meeting I was clear that I wasn't able to get in at that time and either I was happy to join if they shifted it to 8.30 or I would catch up when I got in and get the update on the discussions."

"When I'm not away travelling for work, I've been clear with my team that I'm not available between 5.30 and 7.00pm as that's the time I'm at home putting my son to bed. They know I can be contacted later in the evening and if there was a real emergency they could call me, but in reality there's virtually nothing that can't wait for 90 minutes."

If you are working from home this also includes being clear with members of your family, or those you're living with, when you can and can't be interrupted. This helps reduce the levels of work-family conflict. To help manage your boundaries it's also important to give yourself permission to stick to whatever boundaries you've set yourself and feel ok about saying no.

Am I an integrator or separator?

Most of us have a natural preference for whether we integrate or separate our home and work life. For example, if you are more of an integrator then you are more likely when in the office to be happy to leave and then pick up work later at home, whilst a separator would prefer to stay later and finish their work to then have a free evening. Similarly, if working from home, an integrator is happy to take an extended break and pick up their work later on, whilst a separator would prefer to keep going and then pack up and finish for the day, taking their break then. If you receive a call or discuss work during your weekend or evening, for an integrator then it's less likely to feel like an intrusion, whereas for a separator it may well do.

> *"Just before I went to sleep my partner asked me for advice about a workshop he was running the next day. He was then able to roll over and go to sleep, whereas I find it really tricky when work impinges on home, and I then spent the next hour thinking about all the techniques he could use whilst he was happily snoring away."*

In reality most people aren't one or the other but somewhere in-between, but with a preference for how much their home and work life merge together or are kept apart. It doesn't matter what your preference is, and there isn't a benefit of being either type, however, what can be stressful is if you don't act in ways that are consistent with your preferences.

> *"I find it irritating that my husband's laptop is permanently out on the kitchen worktop as it reminds me of work. He seems very happy that he can dip in and out of work, whereas I definitely prefer to finish my work, even if that means working late, so that I can then switch off."*

When more consistently working from home, if you have a natural preference for separating out, you may find it harder because you don't have that natural temporal or spatial segregation which you get from having a separate, away from home, workplace. However, separators are more likely to adopt boundary management techniques to help alleviate their stress levels when home working.

Natural integrators tend to find working from home less stressful overall as they are happier that their work and home life are intertwined. However, as they are less likely to detach from work and find it harder to switch off, they are less likely to recognise and put in place strategies to give themselves time away from work and so can have increased stress levels.

Time management techniques

The final area to consider as part of strategies to help manage the balance, whether you are a working parent or a typical overworked professional, is thinking about ways to manage your time. There are a whole host of time management books which can provide useful guidance on how to efficiently use your time and reduce the sense of feeling overwhelmed. Ones I often recommend to my coaching clients include *Getting things done* by David Allen, *First things first* by Patrick Forsyth, *One thing* by Gary Keller and *Give me Time* by Mind Gym. This book isn't designed to replicate or provide an alternative to these books, but in summary some of the most useful techniques I've consistently shared are:

–   Using to-do lists – Getting clarity on all the areas you need to work on by collating all of your "to do" items in one place, prioritising this list with a separate daily "what needs to be done today" list and physically checking items off.
–   Prioritise using urgent + important – When creating priorities think through the combination of how urgent it is and how important, which helps you focus on which order to do things in (based on urgency) and how long to spend on each (based on importance).
–   Two-minute rule – Avoid double touching by using the two-minute rule to reduce levels of rework. If you can do a task within two minutes e.g. reply to an email, then do it immediately rather than having to pick up the task again.
–   Pomodoro technique[92] – a really helpful technique, developed by Italian Francesco Cerillo, for when you need a period of focus, e.g. to concentrate on something that's trickier or boring. The principle is that you set a timer for 25 minutes and work without interruption and then have a five-minute break. (It's called Pomodoro after the tomato kitchen timers.)
–   Manage interruptions – your ability to concentrate and perform decreases every time you have an interruption, and it takes a while to increase back up to the same level (see diagram below) so think about how you can reduce interruptions through turning off alerts and blocking out time.

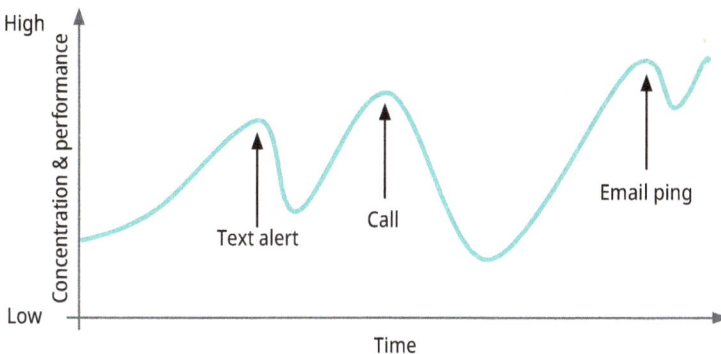

Figure 13: Managing interruptions.

Checklist

Below is a summary of the things to consider either as a returning parent, as the manager of a returning parent, or as someone that needs to think through strategies for managing the balance:

Returner's checklist	√
Where could I get involved in supporting others returning from parental leave?	
What reflections and conversations do I want to have around managing my career?	
If pregnant again, how and when am I'm going to notify others?	
If returning for a second (or subsequent) time, what identity reflections are useful to have?	

Manager's checklist	√
What potential biases or stereotypes may exist for myself or my team and how do I want to tackle them?	
What follow up conversations do I need to have around career progression and balance?	

Strategies to manage the balance checklist	√
If applicable, how effective is home working and what can I put in place to ensure myself or my team are connecting in with each other?	
What tactics do I need to implement for myself or my team to help manage boundaries?	
Am I naturally an integrator or a separator and how do I need to adjust, or help my team adjust, to work with our natural preferences?	
What time management techniques can I put in place for myself or my team to reduce the sense of feeling overwhelmed?	

Afterword

At the beginning of this book I described my own experiences on returning to work and how I hoped the following pages would guide you through this tricky transition, whether as a returning parent or as a manager. I sincerely hope that the various strategies, techniques, experiences of others and checklists have been useful as you think about how to manage going off on parental leave, preparing to return and then adjusting back into the workplace.

The aim of *Returning well* was to produce a comprehensive guide, without turning it into an unwieldly tome; providing the right balance of practical support along with accessible research-based guidance, in a format that's hopefully easy to navigate, wherever you currently are on the journey.

I've been very lucky to have a huge variety of parents, managers, fellow coaches and psychologists who have provided input and critical reviews as this book has progressed. However, things evolve - whether that's legislation, new parental initiatives within organisations, updated psychological research or experiences that haven't been covered. If there are additional things you think should be included or updated within *Returning well*, or other thoughts you have about managing this transition please do get in touch at kirstie@blueacornsolutions.com or via LinkedIn: linkedin.com/in/kirstiesneyd

K J Sneyd

January 2025

https://doi.org/10.1515/9783111618456-007

Acknowledgements

How to thank enough those that have helped me on my journey to getting this book into your hands. My first big shout out is to my two coaching buddies Jane Rosser and Sharon Collier – they have acted as my sounding board, accountability buddies and motivation as I've gone through this journey. Also, a big thanks to Phillipa Kindon who shared her feedback chapter by chapter for the first draft of this book and provided much needed enthusiasm at the early stages of this project.

There is a raft of other people who have either provided those super helpful critical reviews of the book or have given their support in helping to get this book published. These include: Alice Page, Alison Sturgess-Durden, Amy Morse, Anne Priest, Catherine Bruton, Clare Marchant, Liana Slater, Lucy Goode, Patrick Mork, Rebecca Birkbeck, Sally Gupta and Sarah Williment. Apologies if I've left anyone out.

The idea for writing this book was prompted by the research I did whilst at Birkbeck, University of London, so many thanks to my supervisor Kevin Teoh and all the returning parents who took part. This book also couldn't have been written without the insights and reflections from all the other working parents and their managers that I've either interviewed, coached or had discussions with over the years – it's great that your experiences are being shared to help others.

Through the power of LinkedIn I connected in with Matthew Smith from De Gruyter who helped guide me through the publishing process. Many thanks to him and others in the De Gruyter team, especially Ashley Fritsch, who answered my many queries and helped get this book into your hands.

When discussing this section at home over the kitchen table, H, our youngest, asked if they get a mention in here as well – of course you do. The biggest shout out to my family, Bill, Becca and H for all your enthusiasm and support over the years – I genuinely couldn't have done it without you.

https://doi.org/10.1515/9783111618456-008

About the author

Kirstie Sneyd is an organisational psychologist and executive coach, with over 25 years' experience specialising in behaviour change. This book is based on her psychology research from Birkbeck, University of London, her organisational behaviour learnings from her INSEAD MBA and her coaching experience working with parental returners and their managers. Having coached hundreds of professionals through periods of transition, this book draws on Kirstie's practical experience in understanding how to successfully manage through change and maintain a career alongside being a working parent.

Kirstie lives near Bath, Somerset with her husband Bill, dog Millie, and is joined in the university holidays by their two children Becca and H. Aside from her passion for psychology and understanding human behaviour, Kirstie is a keen rower ("crew" for those in the U.S.), cook and traveller.

https://doi.org/10.1515/9783111618456-009

References

1   Carlson, D. S., Grzywacz, J. G., Ferguson, M., Hunter, E. M., Clinch, C. R., & Arcury, T. A. (2011). Health and Turnover of Working Mothers After Childbirth Via the Work-Family Interface: An Analysis Across Time. *Journal of Applied Psychology, 96*(5), 1045–1052.

2   Office for National Statistics. (2021). Families and the labour market. https://www.ons.gov.uk/employmentandlabourmarket/peopleinwork/employmentandemployeetypes/articles/familiesandthelabourmarketengland/2021. Accessed October 2024.

3   Chanfreau, J., Gowland, S., Lancaster, Z., Poole, E., Tipping, S., & Toomse, M. (2011). Maternity and Paternity Rights Survey and Women Returners Survey 2009/10. *Department for Work and Pensions Research Report No.777.*

4   Woolnough, H., & Redshaw, J. (2016). The career decisions of professional women with dependent children: What's changed? *Gender in Management, 31*(4), 297–311.

5   Zhang, J., Thomas, C., Dirr, B., Cone, R., & Spitzmueller, C. (2016). Global Maternity Benefits and Their Impact on Maternal and Child Wellbeing. In R. A. Spitzmueller, C., Matthews (Ed.), *Research Perspectives on Work and the Transition to Motherhood* (pp. 149–169). New York: Springer.

6   Birkett, H., & Forbes, S. (2019). Where's dad? Exploring the low take-up of inclusive parenting policies in the UK. *Policy Studies.*

7   Sneyd, K (2020). Back to work – exploring the experiences of professional maternity returners. *Final dissertation MSc Organisational Psychology, Birkbeck, University of London.*

8   Greenberg, D. N., Clair, J. A., & Ladge, J. (2016). Identity and the transition to motherhood: Navigating existing, temporary, and anticipatory identities. *Research perspectives on work and the transition to motherhood,* 33–55.

9   Chanfreau et al. (2011). See 3.

10   Zippia. (2022). Average paid maternity leave in the US (2022): US Maternity leave statistics, https://www.zippia.com/advice/average-paid-maternity-leave. Accessed October 2024.

11   Sandberg, S. (2013). *Lean in: Women, work, and the will to lead.* Random House.

12   Lean in circles: What are lean in circles? https://support.leanin.org/hc/en-us/articles/360020897654-What-are-Lean-In-Circles-. Accessed October 2024.

13   Chrobot-Mason, D., Hoobler, J. M., & Burno, J. (2019). Lean In versus the literature: An evidence-based examination. *Academy of Management Perspectives, 33*(1), 110–130.

14   Pownall, M., Conner, M., & Hutter, R. R. (2022). Blame it on her 'baby brain'? Investigating the contents of social stereotypes about pregnant women's warmth and competence. *British Journal of Social Psychology, 62*(2), 692–707.

15   Little, L. M., Major, V. S., Hinojosa, A. S., & Nelson, D. L. (2015). Professional image maintenance: How women navigate pregnancy in the workplace. *Academy of Management Journal, 58*(1), 8–37.

16   Okimoto, T. G., & Heilman, M. E. (2012). The "bad parent" assumption: How gender stereotypes affect reactions to working mothers. *Journal of Social Issues, 68*(4), 704–724.

17   Cuddy, Amy J. C, Susan T. Fiske, and Peter Glick. (2004). "When Professionals Become Mothers, Warmth Doesn't Cut the Ice." *Journal of Social Issues,* 60(4): 701–718

18   Hipp, L. (2018). *Damned If You Do, Damned if You Don't? Experimental Evidence on Hiring Discrimination against Parents with Differing Lengths of Family Leave*: October 27, 2020.

19   Kelland, J., Lewis, D., & Fisher, V. (2022). Viewed with suspicion, considered idle and mocked-working caregiving fathers and fatherhood forfeits. *Gender, Work & Organization.*

https://doi.org/10.1515/9783111618456-010

20   Curran, T., & Hill, A. P. (2019). Perfectionism is increasing over time: A meta-analysis of birth cohort differences from 1989 to 2016. *Psychological bulletin, 145*(4), 410–429.

21   Ryan, R. M., & Deci, E. L. (2017). *Self-determination theory: Basic psychological needs in motivation, development, and wellness.* Guilford Publications.

22   Petriglieri, J. (2019). *Couples that work: How dual-career couples can thrive in love and work.* Harvard Business Press.

23   Personnel Today - Flexible working changes. (2024). https://www.personneltoday.com/hr/flexible-working-changes-2024-law-act-legislation-regulations-hr/. Accessed October 2024

24   NHS – Finding an NHS psychological therapies service https://www.nhs.uk/service-search/mental-health/find-a-psychological-therapies-service/. Accessed October 2024.

25   BACP How to find a therapist https://www.bacp.co.uk/about-therapy/how-to-find-a-therapist/. Accessed October 2024.

26   UKCP Overview https://www.psychotherapy.org.uk/about-ukcp/. Accessed October 2024.

27   NHS Overview – Post-natal depression https://www.nhs.uk/mental-health/conditions/post-natal-depression/overview/. Accessed October 2024.

28   NHS overview – see 27.

29   US Department of Health & Human Services – Postpartum depression https://www.womenshealth.gov/mental-health/mental-health-conditions/postpartum-depression. Accessed October 2024.

30   Mayo clinic – Postpartum depression https://www.mayoclinic.org/diseases-conditions/postpartum-depression/symptoms-causes/syc-20376617. Accessed October 2024.

31   NHS – How to care for children with complex needs https://www.nhs.uk/conditions/social-care-and-support-guide/caring-for-children-and-young-people/how-to-care-for-children-with-complex-needs/. Accessed October 2024.

32   American Psychological Association – When your child is diagnosed with a chronic illness https://www.apa.org/topics/chronic-illness/child. Accessed October 2024.

33   Tommy's: Baby loss statistics https://www.tommys.org/baby-loss-support/pregnancy-loss-statistics. Accessed October 2024.

34   Tommy's: Baby loss information and support - https://www.tommys.org/baby-loss-support . Accessed October 2024.

35   MEND – Loss and outreach organisations https://www.mend.org/infant-loss-organizations. Accessed October 2024.

36   Givati, Y. & Troiano, U. (2012). Law, economics, and culture: Theory of mandated benefits and evidence from maternity leave policies. *The Journal of Law and Economics, 55*(2), 339–364.

37   Kornfeind, K. R., & Sipsma, H. L. (2018). Exploring the link between maternity leave and postpartum depression. *Women's Health Issues, 28*(4), 321–326.

38   Canaan, S., Lassen, A., Rosenbaum, P., & Steingrimsdottir, H. (2022). Maternity leave and paternity leave: Evidence on the economic impact of legislative changes in high income countries.

39   Four Day week global case studies. https://www.4dayweek.com/casestudies. Accessed October 2024.

40   Autonomy. (2023). The results are in: The UK's four-day week pilot https://static1.squarespace.com/static/60b956cbe7bf6f2efd86b04e/t/63f3df56276b3e6d7870207e/1676926845047/UK-4-Day-Week-Pilot-Results-Report-2023.pdf. Accessed October 2024.

41   Acceptance and Commitment Therapy. (2022). *Psychology Today*, https://www.psychologytoday.com/us/therapy-types/acceptance-and-commitment-therapy. Accessed October 2024.

42 Acceptance and Commitment Therapy, NHS, https://www.talkingtherapiesportsmouth.nhs.uk/acceptance-commitment-therapy-act. Accessed October 2024.

43 Harris, R. (2019). *ACT made simple: An easy-to-read primer on acceptance and commitment therapy.* New Harbinger Publications.

44 Youtube – World's toughest job interview https://www.youtube.com/watch?v=h0r-I5Djpu8. Accessed October 2024.

45 Iyengar, S. S., & Lepper, M. R. (2000). When choice is demotivating: Can one desire too much of a good thing? *Journal of personality and social psychology, 79*(6), 995–1006.

46 Ladge, J. J., Humberd, B. K., & Eddleston, K. A. (2018). Retaining professionally employed new mothers: The importance of maternal confidence and workplace support to their intent to stay. *Human Resource Management, 57*(4), 883–900.

47 *Gender, Flexibility Stigma and the Perceived Negative Consequences of Flexible Working in the UK – Chung 2018.*

48 EMW Less than a third of eligible men take paternity leave. https://www.emwlaw.com/latest-thinking/less-than-a-third-of-eligible-men-take-paternity-leave/. Accessed October 2024

49 PWC (2016) – Women returners – The £1 billion career break penalty for professional women https://www.pwc.co.uk/economic-services/women-returners/pwc-research-women-returners-nov-2016.pdf. Accessed October 2024

50 WEF (2021) – Global gender gap report https://www3.weforum.org/docs/WEF_GGGR_2021.pdf. Accessed October 2024

51 UNICEF (2019) Business and family-friendly policies https://www.unicef.org/documents/business-and-family-friendly-policies. Accessed October 2024

52 Herman, C. (2009). "It's not the break that's the problem": women SET professionals and career breaks in European companies. In *Women in Science and Technology: Creating Sustainable Careers.* Brussels.

53 Hideg, I., Krstic, A., Trau, R. N., & Zarina, T. (2018). The unintended consequences of maternity leaves: How agency interventions mitigate the negative effects of longer legislated maternity leaves. *Journal of Applied Psychology, 103*(10), 1155–1164.

54 Birkett, H., & Forbes, S. (2019). Where's dad? Exploring the low take-up of inclusive parenting policies in the UK. *Policy Studies.*

55 Fatherhood institute. (2022). Daddy Leave. https://www.fatherhoodinstitute.org/_files/ugd/efff1d_f3da5a6c48d8424187703114601e7b6c.pdf. Accessed October 2024

56 OECD Family database: PF2.1 Parental leave systems https://www.oecd.org/els/soc/PF2_1_Parental_leave_systems.pdf. Accessed October 2024

57 Nakazato, H., Nishimura, J. and Takezawa, J. (2022). 'Japan country note', in Koslowski, A., Blum, S., Dobrotić, I., Kaufmann, G. and Moss, P. (eds.) International Review of Leave Policies and Research 2022. https://www.leavenetwork.org/annual-review-reports/. Accessed October 2024

58 Business Insider. (2018). Sweden is apparently full of "latte dads" carrying toddlers https://www.businessinsider.com/sweden-maternity-leave-paternity-leave-policies-latte-dads-2018-4?r=US&IR=T. Accessed October 2024

59 Guendouzi, J. (2006). The Guilt Thing: Balancing Domestic and Professional Roles. *Journal of Marriage and Family,* 68.

60 Desmond, D., & Meaney, S. (2016). A qualitative study investigating the barriers to returning to work for breastfeeding mothers in Ireland. *International Breastfeeding Journal, 11*(1), 1–9.

61 Gatrell, C. J. (2013). Maternal body work: How women managers and professionals negotiate pregnancy and new motherhood at work. *Human Relations, 66*(5), 621–644.

62   Stumbitz, B., Lewis, S., & Rouse, J. (2018). Maternity management in SMEs: A transdisciplinary review and research agenda. *International Journal of Management Reviews, 20*(2), 500–522.

63   Moffett, J. (2018). "Adjusting to that new norm": How and why maternity coaching can help with the transition back to work after maternity leave. *International Coaching Psychology Review, 13*(2), 62–76.

64   Vitzthum, C. (2017). How can maternity-return coaching complement structural organisational benefits? *International Journal of Evidence Based Coaching & Mentoring, 15*, 44–56.

65   Seignot, N., & Clutterbuck, D. (2016). *Mentoring New Parents at Work: A Guide for Businesses and Organisations*. Routledge.

66   Butts, M. M., Casper, W. J., & Yang, T. S. (2013). How important are work-family support policies? A meta-analytic investigation of their effects on employee outcomes. *Journal of Applied Psychology, 98*(1), 1–25.

67   Business advice (2015) Management of maternity leave troubles small businesses https://businessadvice.co.uk/hr/employment-law/management-of-maternity-leave-troubles-small-businesses/. Accessed October 2024

68   ILO Maternity protection in SMEs, an international review https://www.ilo.org/wcmsp5/groups/public/—dgreports/—dcomm/—publ/documents/publication/wcms_317213.pdf. Accessed October 2024

69   Working families: Small and medium enterprises (SMEs) https://workingfamilies.org.uk/employers/small-and-medium-enterprises-smes/. Accessed October 2024

70   HR Dept (2019) Managing maternity leave https://www.hrdept.co.uk/blog/managing-maternity-leave/. Accessed October 2024

71   Gov.uk Pregnancy and maternity-related discrimination and disadvantage https://www.gov.uk/government/publications/pregnancy-and-maternity-related-discrimination-and-disadvantage-final-reports. Accessed October 2024

72   Personnel Today – Inclusion blow as fewer companies publish parental leave. https://www.personneltoday.com/hr/fewer-employers-publish-parental-leave/. Accessed October 2024

73   CIPD (2018) – Flexible working: the business case. https://www.cipd.co.uk/Images/flexible-working-business-case_tcm18-52768.pdf. Accessed October 2024

74   Mashable (2021) – Iceland ran the world's largest trial of a shorter working week. https://mashable.com/article/iceland-four-day-work-week-trial Accessed October 2024

75   CIPD (2019) - Cross Sector insights on enabling flexible working. https://www.cipd.co.uk/Images/flexible-working-guide-2019-v2_tcm18-58713.pdf. Accessed October 2024

76   Glass, J. L., & Riley, L. (1998). Family Responsive Policies and Employee Retention Following Childbirth. *Social Forces, 76*(4), 1401–1435.

77   McMullan, A. D., Lapierre, L. M., & Li, Y. (2018). A qualitative investigation of work-family-supportive coworker behaviors. *Journal of Vocational Behavior, 107*, 25–41.

78   Bandura, A. (1977). Self-efficacy: toward a unifying theory of behavioral change. *Psychological review, 84*(2), 191–215.

79   Gleason, M. E., Iida, M., Shrout, P. E., & Bolger, N. (2008). Receiving support as a mixed blessing: evidence for dual effects of support on psychological outcomes. *Journal of personality and social psychology, 94*(5), 824–838.

80   Jaeckel, D., Seiger, C. P., Orth, U., & Wiese, B. S. (2012). Social support reciprocity and occupational self-efficacy beliefs during mothers' organizational re-entry. *Journal of vocational behavior, 80*(2), 390–399.

81   Heilman, M. E., & Okimoto, T. G. (2008). Motherhood: a potential source of bias in employment decisions. *Journal of applied psychology, 93*(1), 189.

82 ACAS Managing your employee's maternity leave and pay https://www.acas.org.uk/managing-your-employees-maternity-leave-and-pay. Accessed October 2024.

83 Ogden, J., & Bolton, P. (2014). The role of stage of motherhood, work commitment and identity on the well-being of professional women. *Journal of Arts and Social Sciences, 1*(1), 2.

84 Junker, N. M., Bark, A. S. H., & Gloor, J. L. (2020). Career progression: Left out of the game? In *Navigating the Return-to-Work Experience for New Parents* (pp. 81–88). Routledge.

85 Allen, T. D., Merlo, K., Lawrence, R. C., Slutsky, J., & Gray, C. E. (2021). Boundary management and work-nonwork balance while working from home. *Applied Psychology, 70*(1), 60–84.

86 Elbogen, E. B., Lanier, M., Griffin, S. C., Blakey, S. M., Gluff, J. A., Wagner, H. R., & Tsai, J. (2022). A national study of zoom fatigue and mental health during the COVID-19 pandemic: Implications for future remote work. *Cyberpsychology, Behavior, and Social Networking, 25*(7), 409–415.

87 Nandhakumar, J., & Baskerville, R. (2006). Durability of online teamworking: patterns of trust. *Information Technology & People, 19*(4), 371–389.

88 Psychology today. What is the reciprocity ring https://www.psychologytoday.com/us/blog/the-healing-crowd/201308/what-is-the-reciprocity-ring. Accessed October 2024.

89 Grant, A. (2013). *Give and take: A revolutionary approach to success.* Penguin.

90 Elbogen, E. B., Lanier, M., Griffin, S. C., Blakey, S. M., Gluff, J. A., Wagner, H. R., & Tsai, J. (2022). A national study of zoom fatigue and mental health during the COVID-19 pandemic: Implications for future remote work. *Cyberpsychology, Behavior, and Social Networking, 25*(7), 409–415.

91 Tietze, S., Musson, G., & Scurry, T. (2009). Homebased work: a review of research into themes, directions and implications. *Personnel Review, 38*(6), 585–604.

92 Cerillo, F. The pomodoro technique https://www.pomodorotechnique.com/. Accessed October 2024.

Index

https://doi.org/10.1515/9783111618456-011